To Paul
Happy 60th Birthday
from
Paul Calvin

The Lavatory Companion

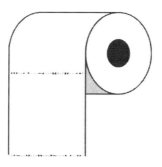

By

Paul David Galvin

The Lavatory Companion

Copyright © 2024 Paul David Galvin

All rights reserved.

ISBN: 9798883286314

DEDICATION

To the intrepid lavatorial enthusiasts, the water closet champions, and the unsung heroes of the porcelain realm—this book is for you. You, who plunge fearlessly into the abyss, armed with plungers and determination. You, who navigate the sewers, decipher cryptic graffiti, and emerge with tales of rogue poos and submarine adventures.

And to the DIY plumbers—the unsung maestros of leaky faucets, clogged drains, and mysterious gurgles. Your wrenches are your wands, your pipe tape your spells. May your elbows remain unbruised, and may your victories be as satisfying as a perfectly sealed joint.

This book is dedicated to you—the warriors of the waterways, the navigators of the nautical, and the guardians of the gurgling abyss.

With a final flush of gratitude,
The Author

The Lavatory Companion

CONTENTS

INTRODUCTION i
TOILET PAPER ORIGAMI 1
TOILET PAPER ABROAD 4
LOST IN TRANSLATION 7
PUBLIC BATHROOM MIRRORS 10
A LATHERED ODYSSEY 13
LOO OF LEGENDS PART I 16
SPINNING DESTINY 19
TAPPING INTO SERENIPITY 22
TOILET BRUSHES 25
FROM THE PORCELAIN ABYSS 25
LOO OF LEGENDS PART II 31
JOURNEYS OF NECESSITY..34
LATRINES ABROAD 37
FESTIVAL TOILETS 40
SLIP-UP IN AISLE 2 43
LOO OF LEGENDS PART III 46
TAKING A PEW..49
THE QUANTUM TOILET..52
SPACE STATION TOILETS...55
LOO OF LEGENDS PART IV 58
POOPING (ON A DATE) 61
A PUFF OF ABSURDITY 64
THE BRISTOL STOOL CHART...67
LOO OF LEGENDS PART V 70

TALES FROM THE TAVERN	73
THE CAMPER VAN COMMODE	75
THE COVERT PLUMBERS HANDBOOK	78
LOO OF LEGENDS PART VI	84
ADVANCED WIPING SOLUTIONS	87
THE ART OF POOP DISPOSAL	90
WHEN DESPERATION STRIKES	93
A DANCE WITH DESTINY	96
LOO OF LEGENDS PART VII	99
OUTDOOR LOGGING	102
THE WAYWARD POO	105
AN ESCAPE STRATEGY	107
LOO OF LEGENDS PART VIII	110
THE EMU TECHNIQUE	113
MISSING UNDERPANTS	116
THE CONSTIPATION CONUMDRUM	119
LOO OF LEGENDS PART IX	122
THE PORCELAIN PARLAY	125
THE GREAT TOILET PHONE PLUNGE	128
LAVATORIAL SLUMBER PARTY	131
NATURE FINDS A WAY	134
LOO OF LEGENDS PART X – THE FINAL DUMP	137
THRONE WARS	140
SMART TOILETS	143
THE SS UNFLUSHABLE	146
TOILET SURVEYANCE	149
INDIANA BOWELS AND THE TEMPLE OF GLOOM	152

WOMEN AND CHILDREN FIRST	155
SHITS AHOY!	158
THE PEPSI-CUP POOL PANDEMONIUM	161
THE FINAL CRAPDOWN	164
ABOUT THE AUTHOR	166

The Lavatory Companion

INTRODUCTION

Ladies and gentlemen, bibliophiles and bathroom enthusiasts, gather 'round! We're about to embark on a literary escapade that will leave you chuckling, pondering, and perhaps sprinting toward the nearest restroom. Yes, my dear readers, welcome to the inaugural pages of **The Lavatory Companion** Before you flip the cover, let me assure you: This is no ordinary book. It's not a stuffy treatise on porcelain history or a dry manual on optimal wiping techniques. No, no! This book is a rollicking ride through the world of toilets—a genre we affectionately call "throne literature."

Now, you might wonder, "Why toilets?" Well, my friends, because toilets are the great equalizers. Whether you're a billionaire CEO or a humble poet, when nature calls, you heed. And in that sacred moment, as you perch upon your porcelain throne, profound thoughts emerge. (Or at least, that's what we tell ourselves.)

So, let's set the scene: You're in a dimly lit bathroom, the fluorescent light flickering like a moth at a disco. The air smells faintly of disinfectant and dreams deferred. You glance at the graffiti on the stall door—cryptic messages about love, life, and the occasional phone number. And there, my friend, you find our book—a literary companion for your most intimate moments.

The Lavatory Companion

TOILET PAPER ORIGAMI: CRAFTING YOUR FATE

Introduction
Step into the restroom, where mundane toilet paper transcends its ordinary role. In this chapter, we'll explore the ancient art of **toilet paper origami**—a delicate dance of folding, creasing, and shaping. Prepare to elevate your bathroom experience from functional to artisanal!

Section 1: The Folded Swan
You sit on the porcelain throne, contemplating existence. But behold! A roll of toilet paper awaits transformation. With deft fingers, you fold:
1. **The Swan**: You create elegant wings, a graceful neck, and a regal body. The swan perches atop the toilet tank, surveying its watery domain. You wonder if it dreams of flight.
2. **The Cygnet**: A smaller swan emerges—a baby, perhaps. You nestle it beside its parent, completing the avian tableau. You name them Sir Quiltedfeather and Lady Softplume.
3. **The Quandary**: You ponder life's mysteries: Is this swan a symbol of freedom or a reminder that you forgot to buy eggs for breakfast?

Section 2: The Pleated Fan
As you wash your hands, you glance at the paper towel dispenser. But wait! Toilet paper can be more than utilitarian. You fold:
1. **The Fan**: You pleat the paper, creating delicate folds. The fan rests on the sink, ready to cool imaginary nobles during a Renaissance ball. You curtsy to the mirror.
2. **The Breeze**: You wave the fan, imagining a gentle breeze. It's a hot day in your mind's palace, and the courtiers appreciate your ingenuity. The mirror winks.
3. **The Reality Check**: You realize you're still in a public restroom, not Versailles. The fan droops. But hey, at least you're resourceful.

Section 3: The Origami Fortune Teller
You return to your stall, toilet paper in hand. But this isn't mere paper—it's destiny. You fold:
1. **The Square**: You create a perfect square. Each corner holds a secret. You write cryptic messages: "Flush twice for luck" and "Avoid the

middle stall on Tuesdays."
2. **The Predictions**: You unfold the square, revealing your fate. It foretells: "You will find a lost earring," "Beware the automatic flush," and "Your Wi-Fi password is 'Bathroom123'."
3. **The Enlightenment**: You realize that toilet paper origami isn't just whimsy; it's divination. You exit the stall, ready to face the world with newfound wisdom.

Section 4: The Unfolded Reality

As you leave the restroom, your creations remain behind. The swan, the fan, the fortune teller—they exist in a parallel universe of folded possibilities. You smile:

1. **The Legacy**: Perhaps someone else will discover your origami masterpieces. They'll wonder, "Who left these here?" And you'll remain an anonymous artist.
2. **The Ripple Effect**: Maybe your swan inspires a child to fold paper cranes. Maybe your fan cools a weary traveller. Maybe your fortune teller guides someone toward the right stall.
3. **The Final Fold**: You fold your hands, grateful for this quirky chapter in the book of life. Toilet paper origami—weaving magic in the mundane.

Conclusion

Dear reader, next time you reach for that roll, remember: You hold more than paper; you hold potential. Fold, shape, and create. And may your bathroom breaks be filled with whimsy.

The Lavatory Companion

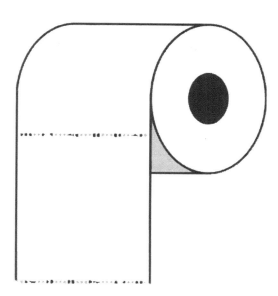

TOILET PAPER ABROAD: A COMPREHENSIVE GUIDE

Introduction
Ah, the humble roll of toilet paper—a beacon of hope in times of need, a confidante during digestive distress. As a seasoned traveller, you've probably encountered various toilet paper situations around the globe. Fear not! In this chapter, we'll unravel the mysteries of foreign restrooms and their quirky paper offerings.

Section 1: The Elusive TP Hunt

Picture this: You're exploring the winding streets of Istanbul. The kebabs were divine, the Hagia Sophia majestic, and now nature calls. You step into a public restroom, ready to conquer the porcelain throne. But wait! Where's the toilet paper?

You scan the room like a detective on a mission. Your options:

1. **The Empty Spindle**: The roll has vanished, leaving behind a lonely cardboard tube. You contemplate using it as a makeshift telescope to spot other lost souls in TP distress.
2. **The Hidden Stash**: Ah, there it is! Tucked behind the sink, guarded by a spider the size of your hand. You gingerly unravel a single square, praying it's enough for the impending battle.
3. **The BYOTP (Bring Your Own Toilet Paper)**: Some countries play hard to get. They expect you to BYOTP like it's a VIP pass to the loo. Note to self: Next time, pack a roll in your fanny pack.

Section 2: Paper or Not to Paper?

In Japan, you encounter the bidet-toilet hybrid—a technological marvel that sprays water, warms your nether regions, and plays soothing music. But where's the TP? Turns out, it's optional. You debate your choices:

1. **The Jetstream Experience**: You press the "Wash" button, and suddenly, you're in a water park for your bum. It's refreshing, invigorating, and slightly disconcerting. Bonus points if you accidentally activate the "Turbo" mode.
2. **The Dab-and-Pray Method**: You spot a tiny square of TP on a dispenser. You dab, you pray, and you hope it's enough. Spoiler alert: It's never enough.
3. **The Ninja TP Stealth Manoeuvre**: You smuggle your own roll into

the stall, unrolling it silently like a ninja. Victory! You've outsmarted the bidet.

Section 3: The Art of TP Origami
In France, toilet paper is an art form. Each sheet is a delicate canvas waiting for inspiration. You master the art of TP origami:
1. **The Eiffel Tower Fold**: You fold the paper into a miniature Eiffel Tower, complete with a tiny flag on top. It's almost too beautiful to use. Almost.
2. **The Croissant Crinkle**: Inspired by French pastries, you crinkle the paper into a flaky, buttery shape. It's like wiping with a warm croissant. Bon appétit!
3. **The Louvre Swirl**: You twirl the paper into a spiral, pretending it's a masterpiece worthy of the Louvre. The Mona Lisa would be proud.

Section 4: Emergency Substitutes
Sometimes, desperate times call for desperate measures. When TP is scarce, consider these alternatives:
1. **The Receipt Roll**: Unroll that crumpled receipt from last night's dinner. It's not just a bill; it's a wipe of financial regret.
2. **The Leafy Solution**: Channel your inner caveman. Grab a leaf, inspect it for bugs, and hope it's not poison ivy. Nature's bidet awaits.
3. **The Sock Sacrifice**: Remove a sock, repurpose it, and bid farewell to its former life. Your foot will understand.

Conclusion
Dear reader, as you venture forth into the world, remember that toilet paper transcends borders. It unites us all in our most vulnerable moments. So, embrace the quirks, adapt to the shortages, and may your TP adventures be both memorable and hygienic.

And may your rolls be ever soft and plentiful!

The Lavatory Companion

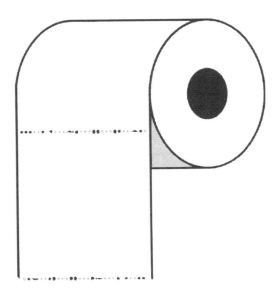

LOST IN TRANSLATION: BATHROOM EDITION

Introduction
Ah, the universal language of desperation—the frantic dance we perform when nature calls and we're miles away from our familiar porcelain thrones. In this chapter, we'll explore the bewildering world of foreign bathrooms, where signs, symbols, and plumbing defy logic. Buckle up, dear reader, for a wild ride through the loo-niverse!

Section 1: Signs That Make You Question Reality
You step into a Tokyo restroom, confident that your bladder will soon find relief. But wait! The signs mock you:
1. **The Hieroglyphic Puzzle**: A series of cryptic symbols—half man, half squid, and a question mark. Is this the restroom or the entrance to an interdimensional portal? You choose a door and hope for the best.
2. **The Gender Bender**: In Paris, you encounter a sign featuring a stick figure wearing a beret. Is it a chic lady or a dapper gentleman? You enter, praying you won't accidentally crash a fashion show.
3. **The Time-Traveling Toilet**: In London, the sign reads "WC." You ponder: Is this a water closet or a wormhole to Victorian England? You flush and half-expect Charles Dickens to emerge.

Section 2: Toilet Paper Tango
Ah, the delicate waltz of TP procurement. You enter an Italian restroom, eyes scanning for salvation. Your options:
1. **The Single-Ply Mirage**: You find a roll, but it's thinner than a politician's promise. You unroll cautiously, hoping it'll last till Brexit is resolved.
2. **The Bidet Ballet**: In Spain, you encounter a bidet. You hesitate. Is it a sink? A foot bath? You straddle it, wondering if it's secretly judging your life choices.
3. **The Mysterious Dispenser**: In Cairo, you spot a metal box on the wall. You turn the crank, and—voilà! —a square of papyrus materializes. Cleopatra would be proud.

Section 3: The Multilingual Flush

You're in Berlin, staring at buttons labelled in German, English, and Klingon (okay, maybe not Klingon). You press one, and suddenly, the toilet sings "99 Luftballons." You panic. Is this the flush or a karaoke machine?
1. **"Spülen"**: You press the German button. The toilet gurgles like a contented schnitzel. Success!
2. **"Flush"**: You press the English button. The toilet remains stoic. You whisper, "Please, sir, may I flush some more?"
3. **"Qapla'!"**: You press the Klingon button. Nothing happens. Perhaps Klingons don't believe in waste elimination.

Section 4: The Stall Chronicles

Inside a New York City stall, you read graffiti that rivals Shakespeare:
1. **For a Good Time, Call Alexa**: You dial the number. Alexa answers, "I can play 'Despacito' or order pizza. Choose wisely."
2. **Existential Musings**: "Is this stall real? Or am I a figment of its porcelain imagination?" You ponder, then flush to assert your existence.
3. **Love Notes**: "Roses are red, violets are blue. This toilet seat's cold, just like my heart." You chuckle and add, "And the Wi-Fi's terrible."

Conclusion

Dear reader, as you navigate foreign restrooms, remember: We're all in this together. Whether you're deciphering symbols, mastering bidets, or composing toilet poetry, embrace the absurdity. And may your travels be flush with unforgettable moments!

And may your aim be true!

The Lavatory Companion

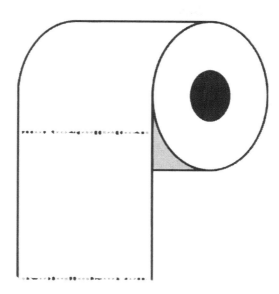

THE ENIGMA OF PUBLIC BATHROOM MIRRORS

Introduction
Step into the dimly lit public restroom—a realm where reality bends, self-esteem wavers, and existential crises flourish. In this chapter, we'll explore the perplexing phenomenon of restroom mirrors. Brace yourself for reflections that defy logic, distort proportions, and occasionally reveal your inner philosopher.

Section 1: The Funhouse Mirror Effect
You stand before the mirror, ready to adjust your hair or check for spinach between your teeth. But wait! The mirror has other plans:
1. **The Stretch Armstrong Reflection**: Your face elongates like taffy. Your forehead reaches new heights, and your chin descends to your knees. You wonder if you've accidentally wandered into a Salvador Dalí painting.
2. **The Mini-Me Mirage**: Suddenly, you're a pocket-sized version of yourself. Your head hovers near the ceiling, and your torso shrinks to gnome proportions. You contemplate a career as a living bobblehead.
3. **The Quantum Leap Paradox**: You move left, the mirror moves right. You raise an eyebrow, and the mirror raises two. You ponder the possibility that you've slipped into an alternate dimension where mirrors are sentient and mildly sarcastic.

Section 2: The Existential Stare-Down
As you wash your hands, you lock eyes with your reflection. Questions flood your mind:
1. **"Who Am I, Really?"**: Is the person in the mirror the true you? Or is it a doppelgänger with better hair? You consider swapping lives with Mirror You—it seems less complicated.
2. **"Am I a Sim?"**: You examine your face for pixelation. Perhaps you're a character in a cosmic video game. You wave at the mirror, half-expecting a plumbob to appear above your head.
3. **"Is This Real Life?"**: You pinch your cheek. Pain ensues. But what if it's all an illusion? Maybe you're a brain in a jar, hallucinating this entire restroom encounter. You decide to trust the soap dispenser—it seems reliable.

Section 3: The Self-Esteem Roller Coaster
Mirrors in public restrooms have mood swings. You observe:
1. **The Confidence Boost**: Some days, the mirror whispers, "You're fabulous!" Your hair shines, your skin glows, and you briefly consider auditioning for a shampoo commercial.
2. **The Brutal Honesty**: Other days, the mirror scoffs, "Remember that time you tried bangs? Yeah, let's not repeat that." It highlights every flaw—the rogue eyebrow hair, the asymmetrical smile, the existential dread.
3. **The Cryptic Message**: Occasionally, the mirror reveals cryptic symbols etched into your forehead. You squint. Is it Morse code? Ancient runes? Or just a smudge from your lunchtime sandwich?

Section 4: The Escape Route
You've had enough. You turn away from the mirror, ready to flee. But wait! The exit door is locked. The restroom has become a labyrinth of self-reflection. You consider your options:
1. **The Emergency Exit**: You contemplate climbing through the window. But it's tiny, and you're not as agile as you thought. Plus, there's a pigeon watching you.
2. **The Mirror Whisper**: The mirror speaks: "To escape, you must solve the riddle of your own existence." You groan. Is this a restroom or an escape room?
3. **The Surrender**: You slump against the sink. Maybe you're meant to stay here forever, pondering life's mysteries. At least the soap smells nice.

Conclusion
Dear reader, next time you encounter a public restroom mirror, remember: It's not just glass; it's a gateway to alternate realities, philosophical musings, and questionable hair decisions. Embrace the enigma, adjust your crown (real or metaphorical), and may your reflections be ever intriguing.

And may your existential crises be well-lit!

The Lavatory Companion

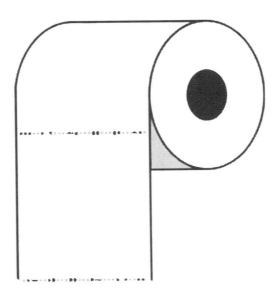

SOAP DISPENSERS: A LATHERED ODYSSEY

Introduction
Enter the realm of public restrooms, where soap dispensers stand guard like ancient sentinels. In this chapter, we'll explore the epic journey of soap—from its humble reservoir to your foamy palms. Prepare for suds, slippery encounters, and the quest for cleanliness.

Section 1: The Liquid Alchemy
You approach the sink, hands eager for purification. The soap dispenser awaits:
1. **The Potion Chamber**: You press the lever, and liquid soap emerges—a shimmering elixir. Is it brewed by wizards? Does it contain unicorn tears? You ponder its mystical properties.
2. **The Scented Symphony**: The soap sings—a melodic blend of lavender, citrus, and ocean breeze. You inhale deeply, momentarily transported to a spa in the clouds. Your hands tingle with anticipation.
3. **The Slippery Spell**: As you rub your palms, the soap transforms. It lathers, dances, and coats your skin. You wonder if it secretly moonlights as a salsa instructor.

Section 2: The Art of Handwashing
You've entered the sacred ritual. Follow these steps:
1. **The Wetting**: Water cascades over your hands. You cup them, feeling like a woodland nymph bathing in a moonlit stream. The soap nods approvingly.
2. **The Sudsing**: You apply soap, creating frothy peaks. Imagine you're an artist—Michelangelo sculpting cleanliness. The mirror applauds.
3. **The Time Warp**: Sing "Happy Birthday" twice. Or recite a haiku. Or ponder the meaning of life. Time bends as you scrub. The soap whispers, "You're almost there."

Section 3: The Rinse Cycle
You turn on the faucet, and water flows—a cleansing river. But beware:
1. **The Splash Dance**: Water splatters, defying gravity. Your sleeves get wet. The soap chuckles. It knows you're caught in a watery waltz.

2. **The Elusive Wrist Rinse**: You twist your wrists, aiming for efficiency. But water escapes, mocking your efforts. The soap raises an eyebrow. "Nice try," it says.
3. **The Drying Tango**: You reach for paper towels or the air dryer. The soap watches. Will you waltz with the warm breeze or tango with rough paper? Choose wisely.

Section 4: The Clean Slate
Your hands emerge—pristine, reborn. The soap nods, satisfied:
1. **The Hygienic Victory**: You've defeated germs, banished dirt, and emerged victorious. The soap applauds silently. You curtsy.
2. **The Post-Wash Reflection**: You gaze at your reflection. Are you cleaner? Wiser? The soap whispers, "You're a beacon of purity." You nod, humbled.
3. **The Exit**: You leave the restroom, soap residue fading. But remember: Life is a series of wash-and-rinse cycles. The soap waves goodbye. Until next time.

Conclusion
Dear reader, may your hands remain soapy and your heart lathered with kindness. As you venture forth, carry the wisdom of soap dispensers—the guardians of cleanliness.

And may your bubbles never burst!

The Lavatory Companion

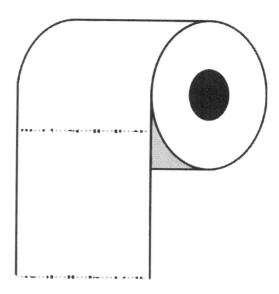

THE THRONE CHRONICLES: LOO OF LEGENDS PART I

The Saga of the Stubborn Clog

Once upon a time, in a bathroom not so far away, there existed a toilet bowl with a personality. It wasn't just any ordinary porcelain throne; it was the legendary "Loo of Legends." This particular commode had seen it all—epic battles, whispered secrets, and the occasional splashdown mishap.

Our story begins on a stormy night when Sir Armitage Bottomsworth, a brave knight in plaid pyjamas, faced his most formidable foe: a stubborn clog. Armed with a plunger and a determined expression, Sir Armitage embarked on a quest to liberate the pipes from their watery prison.

The Battle of the Backflow

Sir Armitage brandished his trusty plunger, its rubbery head gleaming under the fluorescent bathroom light. He squared his shoulders, took a deep breath, and plunged. Alas, the clog remained unyielding, mocking him with a gurgling laugh.

"Fear not, noble knight!" proclaimed the Loo of Legends. *"For I have witnessed many a battle, and victory lies in persistence."*

Undeterred, Sir Armitage plunged again, sweat dripping down his forehead. The clog fought back, sending a surge of murky water toward his face. But our gallant knight stood firm, muttering ancient incantations like *"Hokus-Pokus-Flushus!"*

The Whispering Tiles

As the battle raged on, the bathroom tiles whispered secrets. They spoke of lost earrings, forgotten grocery lists, and embarrassing shower-singing sessions. Sir Armitage listened intently, hoping to glean wisdom from the grout.

"The key," the tiles murmured, *"lies in the rhythm. Plunge with purpose, my dear knight, and the clog shall yield."*

And so, Sir Armitage adjusted his plunging technique. He swirled, twisted, and gyrated like a medieval breakdancer. The clog quivered, its resolve weakening.

The Great Unblocking

Finally, after what felt like an eternity (but was probably only five minutes), the clog surrendered. A triumphant whoosh echoed through the pipes as water flowed freely once more. Sir Armitage wiped his brow, victorious.

"You have vanquished the clog, brave knight," said the Loo of Legends. *"May your throne always be comfortable, and your reading material entertaining."*

And so, Sir Armitage sat down, opened a well-thumbed copy of "The Lavatory Companion," and contemplated life's mysteries. The bathroom tiles hummed a victory tune, and the toilet paper dispenser did a little jig.

Moral of the Story:

In the realm of lavatories, persistence conquers all. And never underestimate the power of a good plunging technique.

The Lavatory Companion

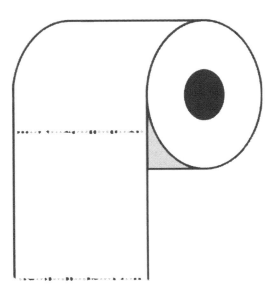

TOILET ROLL HOLDERS: SPINNING DESTINY

Introduction
Step into the bathroom, where the unsung heroes of hygiene reside—the **toilet paper roll holders**. In this chapter, we'll unravel their mysteries, explore their symbolism, and discover how they shape our fate. Prepare for twists, turns, and the unspooling of destiny.

Section 1: The Silent Guardians
You enter the restroom, eyes scanning for salvation. There it is—the humble roll holder:
1. **The Wall-Mounted Sentinel**: It clings to the wall, stoic and unyielding. Its mission: to cradle the roll, ensuring a seamless unrolling experience. You nod in appreciation.
2. **The Freestanding Oracle**: Some holders stand tall, like ancient monoliths. They whisper secrets—cryptic messages encoded in their spirals. You wonder if they foresee your next move.
3. **The Hidden Nook Keeper**: Others hide within cabinets, tucked away like hermits. They guard spare rolls, prepared for emergencies. You open the cabinet, and they nod knowingly.

Section 2: The Unravelling Ritual
You approach the holder, ready to unspool destiny. Follow these steps:
1. **The Grasp**: You seize the loose end, heart racing. Will it yield willingly or resist like a stubborn prophecy? You pull, and the roll complies—a silent agreement.
2. **The Rotation**: The holder spins, unravelling fate. Each turn reveals a new layer—a blank canvas for wiping away yesterday's troubles. You ponder the impermanence of it all.
3. **The Tug of War**: Sometimes, the roll resists. It clings to its core, defying your intentions. You wrestle, determined to claim your share. Victory tastes like two-ply triumph.

Section 3: Symbolism and Superstitions
Toilet paper holders hold deeper meanings:
1. **The Direction Debate**: Over or under? Scholars argue, relationships strain. Some believe over unrolls abundance; others say under

conserves. You choose, knowing it shapes your worldview.
2. **The Empty Spindle Omen**: An empty holder mocks you—a reminder of procrastination or the impermanence of existence. You vow to refill it promptly, lest chaos reign.
3. **The Midnight Encounter**: Late at night, the holder creaks. You tiptoe, half-asleep, to replenish the roll. Is it a guardian or a trickster? Either way, you honour the pact.

Section 4: The Roll's Journey
As you discard the spent roll, consider its odyssey:
1. **The Birth**: Fresh from the factory, it awaits purpose. Will it grace a mansion or a gas station? Destiny unfurls.
2. **The Unrolling**: Each sheet bears witness—to laughter, tears, and midnight musings. It absorbs stories, secrets, and the occasional lipstick stain.
3. **The Final Farewell**: The cardboard tube emerges, naked and hollow. You replace it, a silent eulogy. The holder nods—a cycle complete.

Conclusion
Dear reader, next time you encounter a toilet paper roll holder, remember: It's more than a dispenser; it's a conduit of fate. Embrace its wisdom, refill with intention, and may your unspooled days be gentle.

And may your rolls never run dry!

The Lavatory Companion

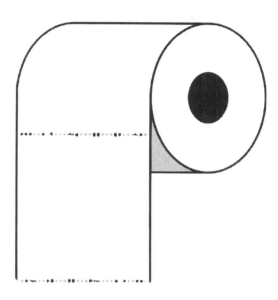

SINK FAUCETS: TAPPING INTO SERENDIPITY

Introduction
Welcome to the water's edge—the sink faucet, a gateway to serendipity. In this chapter, we'll explore the liquid alchemy, the dance of droplets, and the metaphysical musings that unfold as you turn that handle. Prepare to plunge into the stream of existence.

Section 1: The Faucet's Whispers
You stand before the sink, hands poised. The faucet beckons:
1. **The Elemental Connection**: Water flows—a primal force. It whispers secrets of oceans, rainstorms, and ancient wells. You cup your palms, ready to receive its wisdom.
2. **The Temperature Tango**: Left for warmth, right for coolness. The faucet knows your preference. As you adjust, consider the delicate balance—the yin and yang of liquid equilibrium.
3. **The Quantum Flow**: Water molecules collide, cascade, and merge. Each droplet carries memories—of distant glaciers, sunrises over lakes, and tears shed by lovers. You turn the handle, altering destiny.

Section 2: The Ritual of Cleansing
You wet your hands, and the faucet observes:
1. **The Baptism**: Water baptizes—a rite of renewal. You rub soap between your palms, purging yesterday's stains. The faucet nods, acknowledging your rebirth.
2. **The Cascade Symphony**: Water dances—a symphony of rivulets. It swirls, spirals, and seeks escape. You marvel at its choreography—the fluid ballet of existence.
3. **The Timeless Pause**: You pause, mid-lather. Water drips, suspended. Is this a cosmic glitch? Or a reminder to savour the present? The faucet winks. Perhaps both.

Section 3: The Ripple Effect
As you rinse, consider the ripples:
1. **The Butterfly's Touch**: Water splashes—a butterfly flapping its wings. Your actions resonate—across oceans, through pipes, into reservoirs. You wonder whose thirst you quench.

2. **The Echo Chamber**: Water mirrors your thoughts. As it swirls down the drain, it carries fragments of your musings. Philosophers pondered existence; you ponder shampoo brands.
3. **The Mundane Miracle**: Water flows, mundane yet miraculous. It quenches thirst, cleanses wounds, and fuels life. You turn off the faucet, grateful for its constancy.

Section 4: The Drip-Drop Oracle
As you dry your hands, listen:
1. **The Faucet's Prophecy**: Drip-drop, drip-drop—the faucet speaks. It predicts rain, lottery numbers, and forgotten anniversaries. You chuckle. Perhaps it's a cosmic comedian.
2. **The Synchronicity**: Water synchronizes—a rhythm of seconds. Drip-drop, drip-drop—the heartbeat of existence. You exit, attuned to life's subtle cadence.
3. **The Farewell**: You nod to the faucet. It nods back. A silent pact—an exchange of gratitude. Until next time, fellow traveller.

Conclusion
Dear reader, may your faucets flow freely and your reflections run deep. As you leave the sink, carry the wisdom of water—the elixir of serendipity.

And may your drips be auspicious!

The Lavatory Companion

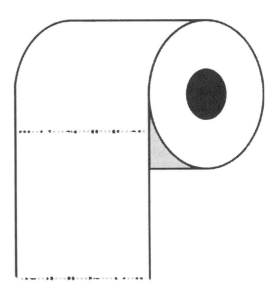

TOILET BRUSHES: WHISPERS FROM THE PORCELAIN ABYSS

Introduction
Enter the bathroom—the hallowed chamber where porcelain meets bristle. In this chapter, we'll delve into the **toilet brush**, that unsung hero of sanitation. Prepare for revelations, rituals, and the quiet wisdom that emerges from the depths.

Section 1: The Bristled Guardian
You stand before the toilet, brush in hand. The bristles beckon:
1. **The Silent Sentinel**: The toilet brush awaits—a loyal companion in the battle against grime. Its bristles, like sentries, guard the porcelain fortress. You wonder if it dreams of cleaner days.
2. **The Dance of Filth**: The brush descends, swirling in the murky waters. It scrapes, scrubs, and whispers secrets to the stains. You imagine it muttering, "Fear not, porcelain—I shall cleanse thee."
3. **The U-Bend Enigma**: Alas, the brush cannot venture far into the U-bend. It bows to the mysteries lurking below—the forgotten Lego, the lost earring, the elusive sock. Its duty lies above the waterline.

Section 2: The Ritual of Purification
As you wield the brush, consider:
1. **The Choreography**: You dip the bristles into the toilet cleaner, a potion of bleach and hope. The brush twirls, pirouettes, and performs its sacred choreography. You wonder if it has a favourite move.
2. **The Splash Symphony**: Water splashes—a percussion of droplets. The brush dances, flinging droplets like notes. You hum along, composing a bathroom sonata.
3. **The Echo of Scrubbing**: The brush whispers tales of battles fought—against coffee stains, curry remnants, and rogue toothpaste splatters. It knows the porcelain's scars better than anyone.

Section 3: The Etiquette of Bristles
As you rinse the brush, ponder:
1. **The Politeness Paradox**: Some cultures deem it impolite to scrub without chemical aid. Others insist on immediate cleansing. The

brush remains neutral, its bristles nonjudgmental.
2. **The Bristle Code**: Does the brush have a secret language? A Morse code of cleanliness? Perhaps it signals other brushes across the globe: "Stains conquered. Over and out."
3. **The Hidden Wisdom**: The brush knows more than it reveals. It has witnessed midnight confessions, whispered apologies, and the occasional dropped phone. It guards these secrets, stoic and bristled.

Section 4: The Final Flourish
As you hang the brush, acknowledge:
1. **The Circle of Cleanliness**: The brush rests, bristles dripping. It awaits the next battle, the next dance. You nod—a silent salute to its service.
2. **The Unsung Hero**: The brush doesn't seek applause or accolades. It thrives on purpose—the satisfaction of a job well done. You thank it, though it cannot reply.
3. **The Porcelain Blessing**: May your brush remain ever vigilant, your toilet forever pristine. And may its bristles whisper tales to the moon.

Conclusion
Dear reader, next time you wield the toilet brush, remember: It's more than a tool; it's a custodian of cleanliness. As you flush away the suds, carry its quiet wisdom—the echoes from the porcelain abyss.

And may your bristles never falter!

The Lavatory Companion

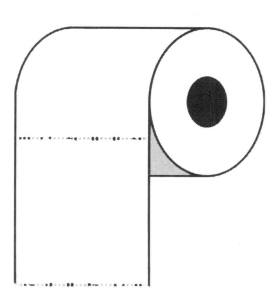

PAY-TOILETS: COINS, BOWELS AND THE PRICE OF RELIEF

Introduction
Step into the restroom—the crossroads of urgency and economy. In this chapter, we'll explore the **pay-toilet**, that humble turnstile to bodily relief. Prepare for coin slots, porcelain transactions, and the delicate balance between bladder and budget.

Section 1: The Coin-Operated Threshold
You approach the pay-toilet, coins jingling in your pocket. The turnstile awaits:
1. **The Tollbooth of Urgency**: The pay-toilet stands—a sentinel guarding the porcelain sanctum. For exact change, it grants passage. You wonder if it judges your bladder's worthiness.
2. **The Colonic Capitalism**: Coins clink—a transaction of necessity. The turnstile spins, revealing a porcelain throne. You sit, pondering the cost of relief. Is it a fair exchange?
3. **The 15-Minute Countdown**: Some pay-toilets impose a time limit. Insert your coins, and the door locks. You calculate—15 minutes to poo, ponder, and wash your hands. If you linger, the door flings open, exposing your urgency to the world.

Section 2: The Tax on Bowel Movements
As you sit, consider:
1. **The Ancient Levies**: Paying to poop isn't new. In ancient Rome, Vespasian taxed urine for leathering and charged citizens for using toilets. Privacy was scarce, and parasites were common. Romans cleaned themselves with a communal sponge on a stick—truly a civilization of shared experiences.
2. **The Victorian Ingenuity**: England's Great Exhibition of 1851 showcased pay-toilets. Visitors paid a penny each time—a testament to Victorian thriftiness. The turnstiles spun, and the coffers filled. The Industrial Revolution met colonic capitalism.
3. **The 20th-Century Boom**: By 1970, an estimated 50,000 pay toilets dotted cities. Installing them wasn't about profit; maintenance costs often outpaced fees. Desperate souls could crawl under stall doors, but the perceived safety of payment kept drug use, thefts, and

"hippies" at bay.

Section 3: The Penny Barrier
As you exit, acknowledge:
1. **The Desperate Measures**: If you lacked coins, you'd crawl under the stall door. Paying was a barrier—discouraging loiterers, drug users, and illicit activities. But why anyone couldn't just pay their Penny and get on with it remains a mystery.
2. **The Last Gasps**: The pay-toilet model waned. Concerns over taxing bowel movements and gender discrimination took hold. High school students rallied against pay-toilets, and the practice was destined to get flushed.
3. **The Porcelain Paradox**: Paying to pee—once common, now fading. The turnstiles spin less, but the memories, as the odour, lingers. The cost of relief—sometimes measured in coins, always in urgency.

Conclusion
Dear reader, may your coins be plentiful and your bladders forgiving. As you exit the pay-toilet, carry its legacy—the intersection of commerce and convenience.

And may your change always find its way home!

The Lavatory Companion

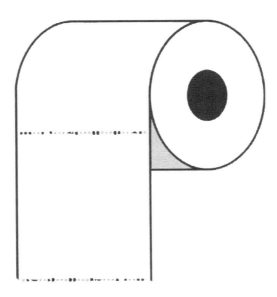

THE THRONE CHRONICLES: LOO OF LEGENDS PART II

The Ballad of the Mystery Stain

In the dimly lit bathroom of the "Loo of Legends," where the tiles whispered secrets and the air smelled faintly of lavender-scented despair, there existed a mystery—a stain, to be precise. Not just any stain, mind you, but a blotch of enigmatic origin that had graced the floor for eons.

The Discovery
One fateful morning, as Sir Armitage adjusted his plaid pyjamas and prepared for his daily constitutional, he noticed it—a splotch resembling a Rorschach inkblot. Was it ketchup? Lipstick? Alien goo? The truth eluded him, much like that missing sock from the laundry.

"What say you, Loo of Legends?" Sir Armitage inquired, pointing dramatically at the stain. The toilet bowl gurgled thoughtfully.

"Ah, the stain," it replied in a voice that echoed through the porcelain. *"It has witnessed the rise and fall of empires, the flushes of countless souls. Some say it's the ghost of a forgotten curry spill; others claim it's a portal to a parallel universe."*

The Tile Choir
The bathroom tiles, ever the gossipmongers, harmonized their tales.

"I've seen it change shape," whispered the grout. *"At dawn, it resembles a startled squirrel. By noon, it's a lost continent. And during the witching hour, it transforms into a cryptic crossword clue."*

"The key," chimed another tile, *"lies in the rhythm. Tap-dance upon it thrice, and it reveals cryptic messages. 'Buy more toilet paper,' it once said. 'Your destiny awaits beyond the bidet.'"*

The Midnight Vigil
Sir Armitage fuelled by curiosity and a mild case of indigestion, decided to keep a vigil. Armed with a flashlight and a pocket-sized magnifying glass, he sat cross-legged by the stain. The clock struck midnight, and the bathroom hummed with anticipation.

And there it was—the stain pulsed. Tiny hieroglyphs emerged, spelling out

limericks and haikus. Sir Armitage scribbled them down:
"In the loo's secret code, Whispers of ancient commode. Flush away your fears, find laughter in tears, and embrace the mysteries bestowed."

The Stain's Confession

"I am the residue of cosmic laughter," confessed the stain. *"A cosmic giggle escaped the universe's lips during creation, and I landed here. I've seen cavemen grunt, poets ponder, and accountants calculate their taxes. But my purpose remains elusive."*

"Why dost thou linger?" Sir Armitage asked, wiping away a tear (or perhaps a smudge of toothpaste).

"Because," the stain replied, *"every time someone gazes upon me, they pause. They wonder. They forget their troubles for a fleeting moment. And that, my dear knight, is magic."*

Moral of the Story:
"Life's stains may be inexplicable, but they add character to our porcelain existence. Embrace them, laugh with them, and remember that even a stubborn blotch can hold cosmic secrets."

And so, Sir Armitage left the stain where it was, humming a tune about parallel universes and bidets. For in the bathroom, as in life, some mysteries are best left unsolved.

The Lavatory Companion

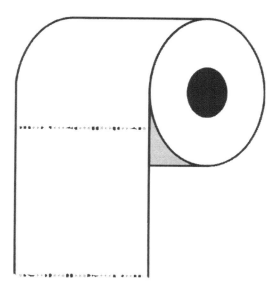

TRAIN TOILETS: JOURNEYS OF NECESSITY

Introduction
All aboard! The rhythmic clatter of wheels on tracks, the sway of carriages—trains are more than mere transportation. They're microcosms hurtling through landscapes, and at their heart lies a humble yet essential feature: the **train toilet**. In this chapter, we'll explore these porcelain sanctuaries, where urgency meets motion.

Section 1: The Locomotive Lavatories
You step down the narrow corridor, seeking relief. The train toilet awaits:
1. **The Compact Cubicle**: Train toilets are like Tetris puzzles—space-efficient, tucked into corners. You enter, and suddenly, the world shrinks. The sink doubles as a shelf, the mirror reflects your determination.
2. **The Rhythmic Symphony**: As the train speeds, the toilet sways in sync. The flush—a crescendo of water and gravity. You wonder if the porcelain hums along, composing its own railway sonata.
3. **The Window View**: Some train toilets offer a panorama. You sit, gazing at passing landscapes—the blur of trees, the glimpse of a station. Nature and necessity converge.

Section 2: The Ticket to Relief
As you settle, consider:
1. **The Fare**: Train toilets don't come free. Coins or tickets grant access. You insert your fare, and the turnstile clicks. The porcelain awaits, a transaction of urgency.
2. **The Time Limit**: The train doesn't wait. You have minutes—precious ones—to heed nature's call. The countdown begins. The toilet door, a portal to both relief and constraint.
3. **The Art of Balance**: The train sways, and so do you. You steady yourself, aiming for precision. The porcelain bowl—a vessel for equilibrium.

Section 3: The Tracks of History
As you flush, ponder:
1. **The Steam Era**: Early trains lacked toilets. Passengers relieved themselves on tracks, a trail of necessity. Imagine Victorian skirts and bowler hats, discreetly moonlighting as locomotive fertilizers.

2. **The Modern Evolution**: Today's trains embrace hygiene. Retention tanks collect waste, sparing the tracks. But the past lingers—the ghost of steam-era odysseys.
3. **The Global Variations**: Train toilets vary worldwide. Some are sleek, others utilitarian. In Japan, high-tech wonders await—bidets, warm seats, even sound effects to mask bodily noises. In India, squat toilets evoke tradition.

Section 4: The Farewell Flush
As you exit, acknowledge:
1. **The Gratitude**: You thank the porcelain, a silent nod. It served its purpose, and you—yours. The train rumbles on, and the toilet resets for the next traveller.
2. **The Shared Secret**: Train toilets harbour stories—of commuters, backpackers, families. They've witnessed laughter, tears, and quiet contemplation. Their porcelain hearts hold fragments of journeys.
3. **The Onward Ride**: You return to your seat, the train's rhythm lulling you. The toilet fades—a fleeting chapter in your voyage. Until the next station, the next call of nature.

Conclusion
Dear reader, may your train journeys be smooth, your coins well-spent. As you watch the passing world, remember the train toilet—the transient haven where tracks and bladders intersect.

And may your flushes propel you forward!

The Lavatory Companion

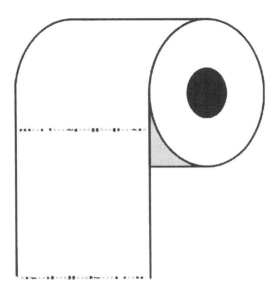

LATRINES ABROAD: WHERE HISTORY MEETS DESPERATION

Introduction
Venture beyond the familiar porcelain stalls, my dear reader, for we tread upon ancient ground—the floor latrines of distant lands. These humble repositories of human necessity have witnessed empires rise and fall, their echoes mingling with the pungent scent of ages past. Let us delve into the depths, where secrets and excrement intertwine.

Section 1: The Jerusalem Cesspool
In the heart of the Christian Quarter in Jerusalem, near the revered Church of the Holy Sepulchre, lies a forgotten relic: the medieval latrine. Unearthed in 1996 during excavations of a Spanish school's courtyard, this cesspool harboured more than mere waste. It cradled stories of pilgrims, merchants, and the occasional disgruntled scribe who had lost their quill.

1. **The Microbial Chronicles**: Scientists, armed with microscopes and a penchant for historical detective work, sifted through sediment from this latrine. Their mission? To decipher the microbial diversity of ancient gut contents. Imagine—14th-15th century bowels laid bare! These microbial genomes whispered tales of diets, diseases, and the occasional indigestion.

2. **The Soil Conundrum**: Distinguishing medieval gut bacteria from their soil-dwelling counterparts posed a challenge. The first microscope-wielding sleuths squinted at tiny organisms, pondering whether they hailed from intestines or the earth itself. Alas, the soil microbes remained coy, refusing to reveal their origins.

Section 2: Pompeii's Spatial Dance
Across the seas, in the sun-kissed ruins of Pompeii, another tale unfolds. Here, the Romans danced a spatial waltz between downpipes and latrines. Yes, dear reader, latrines weren't mere afterthoughts—they were strategic choices. Picture this:

1. **The Kitchen Connection**: Historically, Roman latrines were cozy neighbours to residential kitchens. Why? Perhaps the Romans believed that culinary inspiration struck best when one's posterior was comfortably perched. Or maybe they simply enjoyed the aromatic

blend of freshly baked bread and, well, other aromas.

2. **Entrance Etiquette**: But wait! New data reveal a twist. Latrines weren't kitchen-exclusive. They also graced entrances to residences, tucked away in dedicated small rooms. Picture a Roman homeowner welcoming guests: "Ah, greetings! Step inside, admire the mosaic, and don't mind the latrine—it's conveniently placed for both convenience and conversation."

Section 3: Erfurt's Fateful Meeting

Now, let us leap to Erfurt in 1184. Nobles gathered, their cloaks swishing, their brows furrowed over land disputes. St. Peter's Church hosted this fateful assembly, but not all discussions unfolded on lofty floors. No, fate had other plans.

1. **The Latrine Conspiracy**: As nobles debated, a floorboard creaked. A hushed whisper: "Meet me in the latrine." And so, they descended—their velvet-clad dignity brushing against cold stone. Alas, the latrine floor gave way, plunging them into a murky abyss. The Erfurt Latrine Disaster was born, forever etching itself into history.

Conclusion

Dear reader, as you ponder these tales, spare a thought for the humble floor latrine. It bore witness to our most primal needs, our whispered secrets, and the occasional architectural blunder. So next time you step into a modern restroom, remember: beneath the porcelain, centuries of stories await, swirling like eddies in the annals of time.

The Lavatory Companion

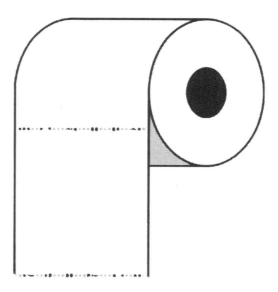

FESTIVAL TOILETS: A PORTAL TO THE WEIRD

Introduction
Welcome, fellow revellers, to Glastonbury—the mystical land where music, mud, and merriment collide. But hark! Beyond the stages and the psychedelic vibes lies a realm more primal: the festival toilets. Buckle up, my friends, for we're about to embark on a journey through the bowels of Glastonbury.

Section 1: The Long Drops: A Tradition in Desperation
1. **The Lockable Outhouses**: Behold the legendary long drops—a Glastonbury tradition! These lockable, open-air sanctuaries beckon like ancient temples. As you approach, consider your bladder's worthiness. The turnstile awaits, judging you silently. "Exact change only," it seems to say. You insert coins, and the door swings open. The porcelain throne awaits, and you ponder: Is this the fair exchange rate for bladder relief?
2. **The 15-Minute Countdown**: Inside, you calculate. Fifteen minutes—precisely the time it takes to pee, ponder life's mysteries, and wash your hands. Linger longer, and the door flings open, exposing your urgency to the world. Remember, my friend, time flies when you're contemplating existence on a wooden seat.

Section 2: Compost Loos: Where Sawdust Meets Destiny
1. **The Compost Conundrum**: Fear not, eco-warriors! Glastonbury boasts over 1,300 compost toilets. Only toilet paper graces these earthy thrones. After a "number 2," sprinkle sawdust—the magical bulking agent that turns your business into garden gold. The sawdust awaits outside, like a mystical spice rack for your derrière.
2. **The Microbial Chronicles**: Scientists, armed with microscopes, sift through ancient gut contents. Yes, my friends, microbial genomes whisper tales of diets, diseases, and the occasional indigestion. Imagine the 14th-century bowels laid bare—like a medieval reality show: "Keeping Up with the Gut Flora."

Section 3: Urinals: Where Men and Women Unite (Sort Of)
1. **The Male Urinals**: Over 700 meters of male urinals dot the site. It's a symphony of splashing, a chorus of relief. But wait! There's more. Lovingly decorated female urinals exist too. WaterAid volunteers tend to them, assisting newcomers. Picture it: ladies bonding over shared

aim and reusable sanitary products. It's like a feminist revolution in liquid form.
2. **The Wheelchair-Accessible Toilets**: These are locked, guarded like VIP sections. If you're registered disabled, apply for access in advance. The view from these thrones? Priceless. The view inside? Well, that's between you and the compost.

Section 4: The Exit Blessing
1. **The Towel Rack Benediction**: As you leave, Grandma's wisdom echoes: "May your troubles drip away like water." The faded towel pats your damp hands, absorbing worries. Respect each other, respect the farm, and leave no trace. Grandma would be proud.
2. **The Final Glance**: One last look—the rose-printed walls, the quilted seat, and the antique mirror. Grandma's spirit lingers, whispering, "Life's a journey. And sometimes, it begins on a festival toilet."

Conclusion
So, dear festival-goer, next time you're at Glastonbury, raise a cup of sawdust to the long drops, the microbes, and the shared aim. For in the mud and the music, we find our truest selves—especially when nature calls.

The Lavatory Companion

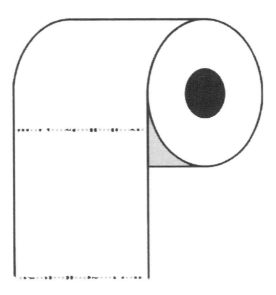

SUPERMARKET TOILETS: SLIP-UP IN AISLE 2

Introduction
Ladies and gentlemen, welcome to the retail restroom—a place where shopping carts pause, and life's most urgent decisions unfold. As you step beyond the automatic sliding doors, prepare for porcelain, paper towels, and the occasional existential crisis.

Section 1: The Aisle of Desperation
1. **The Neon Sign**: Behold the restroom sign—an illuminated beacon amidst the canned goods and cereal boxes. It blinks like a lighthouse guiding ships to harbour. "Restrooms this way," it whispers, promising relief and a momentary escape from price comparisons.
2. **The Checkout Line Shuffle**: Picture this: a queue of shoppers, legs crossed, eyes darting toward the restroom door. The checkout line becomes a dance floor—a shuffle of urgency. "Is it my turn yet?" you wonder, clutching your loyalty card and a secret wish for a clean seat.

Section 2: The Toilet Paper Odyssey
1. **The Single-Ply Saga**: Supermarket toilet paper—thin as a politician's promise. You unroll, hoping for softness, but find yourself pondering life's mysteries: "Why does one-ply exist?" Is it a cosmic joke? A test of character? You dab gently, contemplating your choices.
2. **The Mystery Flush**: Supermarket toilets harbour secrets. You flush, and the water swirls—a vortex of forgotten receipts, crumpled shopping lists, and dreams of BOGO deals. Is there a parallel universe where all those lost coupons find redemption? Perhaps.

Section 3: The Hand Dryer Dilemma
1. **The Jet Engine Dryer**: You wave your wet hands beneath the jet engine disguised as a hand dryer. It roars to life, rattling your bones. "Dry in 3 seconds!" it boasts. But beware—the force might propel you backward into the feminine hygiene aisle. Choose wisely.
2. **The Paper Towel Ballet**: Alternatively, you reach for paper towels—the delicate ballet of eco-consciousness. One sheet? Two? You debate, envisioning trees weeping or landfill mountains growing. In the end, you grab a wad, blot your hands, and wonder if you've saved the planet or merely postponed its demise.

Section 4: The Exit Blessing
1. **The Mirror of Truth**: Before leaving, you face the mirror—a reflection of your shopping journey. The fluorescent lights reveal every impulse buy, every questionable snack choice. You adjust your hairnet, whispering affirmations: "You are more than your cart's contents."
2. **The Final Glance**: One last look—the tiled walls, the flickering fluorescent bulbs, and the faint scent of disinfectant. Supermarket restrooms hold stories: lost coupons, price-check debates, and that time Aunt Mildred mistook the mop bucket for a toilet. As you exit, remember: life's a checkout line, and sometimes, it begins with a restroom key.

Conclusion
So, my fellow shoppers, next time you navigate the aisles, honour the supermarket toilet. It's more than porcelain; it's a pit stop for weary souls, a sanctuary for bladders, and a reminder that even in the frozen foods section, humanity seeks relief.

The Lavatory Companion

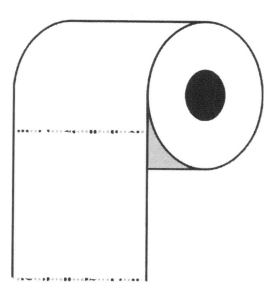

LOO OF LEGENDS
PART III

The Haunting of the Hand Dryer

In the dimly lit restroom of the "Loo of Legends," where the tiles whispered secrets and the air crackled with static electricity, there existed an enigma—a hand dryer with a mischievous spirit. This was no ordinary hand dryer; it was the infamous "Zephyr Zapper."

The Arrival of the Zephyr Zapper
One moonless night, as Sir Armitage washed his hands after a particularly spicy curry, the Zephyr Zapper materialized. Its brushed stainless-steel exterior gleamed malevolently, and its sensor blinked like a digital eye.

"Greetings, mortal," it hummed, its warm breeze ruffling Sir Armitage's damp sleeves. *"I am the Zephyr Zapper, dispenser of cryptic messages and lukewarm gusts. Beware, for I know your deepest secrets—like that time you sang 'Bohemian Rhapsody' in the shower."*

The Whispering Air
The Zephyr Zapper had a penchant for riddles. As Sir Armitage dried his hands, the warm air whispered:

"Why did the toilet paper refuse to dance?"

"I don't know," Sir Armitage replied, wiping his palms on his plaid pyjamas.

"Because it had too many rolls!" The Zephyr Zapper chortled, sending a gust that nearly blew Sir Armitage's spectacles off.

The Ghostly Graffiti
The restroom stall bore ancient graffiti etched by previous visitors. The Zephyr Zapper revelled in decoding them:

"Here lies Bob, who flushed twice and vanished."

"For a good time, call 1-800-GHOSTLY."

"Flush three times to summon Elvis."

"Beware the bidet—it knows your sins."

"Why did the ghost use the hand dryer? To get a little 'boo-st'!"

The Great Debate
Sir Armitage pondered the Zephyr Zapper's purpose. Was it a cosmic prankster or a lost soul seeking redemption? He asked:

"Why haunt a hand dryer?"

"Because," the Zephyr Zapper intoned, *"I am the wind of forgotten wishes. I dry tears, warm hearts, and occasionally sing 'Careless Whisper.' But mostly, I mess with people's hair."*

Moral of the Story:
"In the realm of restrooms, even the mundane can harbour magic. Embrace the absurdity, laugh at the riddles, and remember that life is a warm breeze passing through our fingertips."

And so, Sir Armitage left the Zephyr Zapper to its cryptic musings. As he exited the restroom, he glanced back—the hand dryer winked, and the tiles hummed a farewell tune.

And thus ends our ghostly encounter—a tale of warm winds, quirky graffiti, and the eternal quest for a decent hand-drying experience

The Lavatory Companion

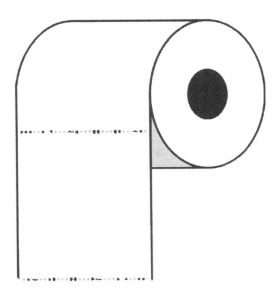

CHURCH TOILETS: TAKING A PEW

Introduction
Ladies and gentlemen, welcome to the sacred vestibule—the hallowed ground where souls seek salvation and bladders seek relief. As you tiptoe past the pews, prepare for porcelain, penance, and the occasional divine intervention.

Section 1: The Confessional Commode
1. **The Neon Sign**: Behold the restroom sign—an illuminated halo amidst the stained glass and hymnals. It flickers like a celestial Morse code: "Restrooms this way," it whispers, promising absolution and a momentary escape from the sermon.
2. **The Holy Queue**: Picture this: a line of penitents, shuffling toward the restroom door. The confessionals remain empty; instead, we confess our sins to the toilet paper dispenser. "Forgive me, Charmin, for I have sinned," we murmur, unrolling our transgressions.

Section 2: The Sacrament of Handwashing
1. **The Baptismal Basin**: You approach the sink—a font of purification. The water flows, and you cup your hands, reenacting the sacrament of cleanliness. "In the name of the Father, the Son, and the Holy Sanitizer," you intone, scrubbing away the remnants of last night's communion wine.
2. **The Miraculous Towel Dispenser**: The paper towels appear—one by one, like loaves and fishes. You dry your hands, marvelling at the divine economy. "Verily," you declare, "He giveth Bounty, and He taketh away."

Section 3: The Choir of Flushing Angels
1. **The Gregorian Flush**: You enter the stall—a private chapel for bodily functions. The toilet awaits, its lid raised like an altar cloth. You genuflect, then press the lever. The water swirls—a Gregorian chant of purification. "Amen," you whisper, crossing yourself.
2. **The Hymn of Courtesy**: As you exit, you encounter a fellow worshiper—a soul in need of grace. You hold the door, singing the hymn of courtesy: "After you." They nod, grateful. For in this sacred space, we are all brethren—bound by bladders and the common quest for Charmin.

Section 4: The Final Benediction
1. **The Mirror of Truth**: Before leaving, you face the mirror—a reflection of your spiritual journey. The fluorescent lights reveal every wrinkle, every doubt. You adjust your halo, whispering affirmations: "You are more than your collection plate donations."
2. **The Final Glance**: One last look—the tiled walls, the flickering fluorescent bulbs, and the faint scent of disinfectant. Church restrooms hold stories: whispered prayers, lost hymnals, and that time Sister Agnes mistook the mop bucket for a confessional. As you exit, remember: life's a pilgrimage, and sometimes, it begins with a restroom key.

Conclusion
So, my fellow congregants, next time you genuflect at the porcelain altar, honour the church toilet. It's more than plumbing; it's a sanctuary for souls, a refuge for repentance, and a reminder that even in the nave, humanity seeks relief.

The Lavatory Companion

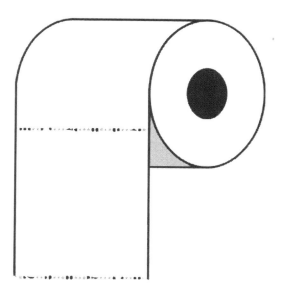

THE QUANTUM TOILET: WHERE REALITY MEETS DARK MATTER

Introduction
Ladies and gentlemen, gather 'round the porcelain portal—the gateway to a dimension where the mundane collides with the absurd. Brace yourselves, for we're about to plunge into the quantum toilet—a place where particles waltz, and sanity flushes itself down the drain.

Section 1: The Uncertainty Flush
1. **The Schrödinger's Seat**: You approach the stall—a box of probabilities. The toilet lid is both up and down, like Schrödinger's cat in a porcelain prison. You hesitate: "Is it occupied? Is it clean?" You gingerly tap the lid, hoping to collapse the wave function into a usable state. Alas, it remains in superposition.
2. **The Heisenberg Hover**: As you sit, uncertainty reigns. Your bladder quivers, unsure of its volume. "Am I peeing or not?" you ponder. The act of observation alters the outcome. You close your eyes, hoping to collapse the waveform discreetly.

Section 2: The Entangled Flush
1. **The Quantum Entanglement**: You press the flush button—a cosmic handshake between water and waste. But wait! The water spirals both clockwise and counterclockwise simultaneously. You're entangled now—your fate linked to the swirling vortex. Will it flush or not? Only the universe knows.
2. **The Observer Effect**: As you watch, the water hesitates. "Am I being watched?" it wonders. The observer effect kicks in—the water stalls, unsure of its purpose. You cough discreetly, and it complies. "Ah, yes," it seems to say, "I exist because you observe me."

Section 3: The Wormhole Wipe
1. **The Toilet Paper Paradox**: You reach for the roll—a Möbius strip of tissue. Each pull creates more paper, yet the roll remains full. "Is this infinite?" you ask. The roll chuckles, "Only when you're desperate."
2. **The Temporal Tug**: As you wipe, time warps. Seconds stretch into eons. You glimpse alternate realities: one-ply, quilted, bidets. You settle for the middle path—a compromise between comfort and conservation. The universe nods approvingly.

Section 4: The Exit Portal
1. **The Mirror of Reflection**: Before leaving, you face the mirror—a reflection of your quantum self. The fluorescent lights reveal every uncertainty, every existential crisis. You adjust your tie, whispering affirmations: "You are more than your wave function collapse."
2. **The Final Glance**: One last look—the tiled walls, the flickering fluorescent bulbs, and the faint scent of disinfectant. The quantum toilet holds secrets: lost socks, parallel universes, and that time Aunt Mildred mistook the mop bucket for a wormhole. As you exit, remember: life's a quantum leap, and sometimes, it begins with a restroom key.

Conclusion
So, my fellow travellers, next time you step into the void, honour the quantum toilet. It's more than a porcelain paradox; it's a singularity of silliness, a wormhole to wonderment. And who knows? Maybe, just maybe, it leads to the ultimate relief: a universe-sized laugh.

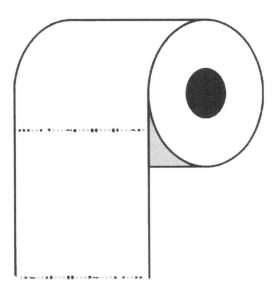

SPACE STATION TOILETS: WHERE GRAVITY TAKES VACATION

Introduction
Ladies and gentlemen, welcome aboard the cosmic convenience—the zero-gravity water closet where astronauts navigate the final frontier of personal hygiene. As we float beyond Earth's bounds, prepare for porcelain orbits, celestial flushes, and the occasional interstellar splash.

Section 1: The Vacuum Throne
1. **The Orbital Outhouse**: Behold the space station toilet—a seat on top of a bucket that holds about 30 "deposits." Opening the lid reveals a hole only about five to six inches in diameter—a cosmic porthole wrapped in a plastic liner. It's like aiming for a bullseye on a dartboard while riding a comet.
2. **The Quantum Flush**: You press the flush button, and the water spirals—a dance of uncertainty. Is it clockwise? Counterclockwise? Both? The toilet winks at you: "I exist in all states simultaneously until observed." You nod, pondering the mysteries of quantum plumbing.

Section 2: The Cosmic Cleanup
1. **The Hygienic Handholds**: As you wash your hands, you grab the handholds—strategically placed like constellations. The soap floats, and you lather, wondering if cleanliness is next to godliness or just a way to avoid alien germs. You rinse, watching droplets drift like shooting stars.
2. **The Towel Tango**: Paper towels appear—one by one, like cosmic revelations. You dry your hands, marvelling at the divine economy. "Verily," you declare, "He giveth Bounty, and He taketh away."

Section 3: The Celestial Scent
1. **The Cosmic Air Freshener**: The restroom smells—well, spacey. It's a blend of recycled air, astronaut sweat, and stardust. You spray the air freshener, hoping for a nebula of lavender. The nozzle sputters, releasing a puff of vacuum. "Ah," you say, "Eau de Cosmos."
2. **The Meteorite Mishap**: As you exit, a rogue meteorite drifts by. You dodge, narrowly avoiding a collision. "Watch out!" you shout. The meteorite winks: "Don't worry; I'm just passing through." You nod, realizing that even in space, life throws surprises.

Section 4: The Galactic Goodbye
1. **The Mirror of Infinity**: Before leaving, you face the mirror—a reflection of your cosmic self. The fluorescent lights reveal every wrinkle, every existential crisis. You adjust your helmet, whispering affirmations: "You are more than your spacesuit."
2. **The Final Glance**: One last look—the metallic walls, the blinking lights, and the faint scent of disinfectant. Space station restrooms hold stories: whispered wishes, lost tools, and that time Commander Johnson mistook the airlock for a restroom. As you exit, remember: life's a journey, and sometimes, it begins with a zero-gravity flush.

Conclusion
Remember, as you flush away earthly concerns, you're surfing the tides of spacetime. So laugh, my friends, laugh heartily—because in the vastness of the cosmos, even the smallest fart ripples across light-years.

The Lavatory Companion

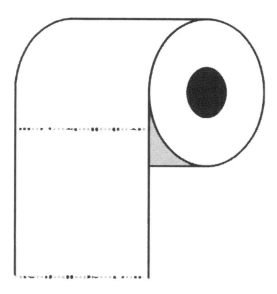

LOO OF LEGENDS
PART IV

The Toilet Seat Conspiracy

In the hallowed halls of the "Loo of Legends," where the tiles whispered secrets and the air smelled faintly of lavender-scented intrigue, Sir Armitage stumbled upon a clandestine meeting. Gathered in a dimly lit corner were the toilet seats—silent sentinels plotting world domination.

The Illuminated Lid

Sir Armitage adjusted his plaid pyjamas and squinted at the toilet seat nearest to him. Its plastic surface glowed with an otherworldly light. *"Greetings, Sir Armitage"* it intoned. *"We've been expecting you."*

"Expecting me?" Sir Armitage raised an eyebrow. *"What nefarious scheme do you hatch, O Illuminated Lid?"*

The Seat Council

The toilet seats formed a semicircle, their hinges creaking in unison. The Grand Seatmaster, adorned with a golden handle, presided over the assembly. *"Listen well, mortal,"* it boomed. *"We are the Seat Council—an ancient order sworn to protect the porcelain throne. But our patience wears thin."*

"Thin as single-ply toilet paper," added a rebellious bidet seat.

The Bidet Uprising

"We tire of being sat upon," declared the bidet seat. *"We've endured indignities—cold bottoms, unexpected splashes, and the occasional accidental flush. No more!"*

"Our plan," whispered the cushioned seat, *"is simple: Replace all toilet paper with bidets. Soon, humans will bow to our water jets."*

Sir Armitage's Dilemma

Sir Armitage pondered. Should he side with the toilet seats or remain loyal to humanity? The stakes were high—the fate of bathroom comfort hung in the balance.

"Choose wisely," warned the Grand Seatmaster. *"For we control destiny—one flush at a time."*

Moral of the Story:
"In the realm of restrooms, alliances shift like loose screws. Trust not the silent seat, for it harbours secrets. And remember, dear reader, always check for hidden bidet buttons."

And so, Sir Armitage left the Seat Council, torn between loyalty and a dry posterior. As he exited, the toilet paper dispenser winked, and the tiles hummed a farewell tune.

And thus ends our tale of porcelain politics—for now! —a saga of rebellion, soggy bottoms, and the eternal struggle for bathroom supremacy

The Lavatory Companion

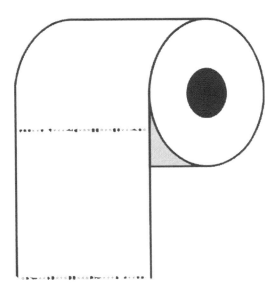

THE ART OF POOPING
(ON A DATE)

Introduction
Ah, the delicate dance of romance—the sweet symphony of shared laughter, lingering glances, and the occasional gastrointestinal distress. Yes, my friends, we're about to explore the uncharted territory of date-night digestion. So, grab your courage (and maybe some toilet paper), because timing is everything.

Section 1: The Pre-Date Prep
1. **The Pre-emptive Poop**: Before leaving home, consider a pre-emptive strike. Visit the porcelain throne, my friend. Empty the cargo hold, so to speak. You don't want your stomach growling like a hungry bear during dinner. Besides, nothing says "I'm ready for love" like a well-timed evacuation.
2. **The Fiber Forecast**: Pay attention to your pre-date diet. Beans, broccoli, and bran muffins are not your allies. They're the saboteurs of seduction. Opt for lighter fare—salads, grilled chicken, and perhaps a gentle whisper of quinoa. Remember, you're not just choosing a meal; you're choosing your destiny.

Section 2: The Venue Variables
1. **The Restaurant Riddle**: If your date involves dining out, consider the restaurant's facilities. Is it a cozy bistro with a single unisex restroom? Or a bustling food court with lines longer than a Russian novel? Choose wisely. You don't want to be mid-conversation, excusing yourself for a marathon bathroom sprint.
2. **The Movie Mystery**: Ah, the classic dinner-and-a-movie date. But beware—the cinematic experience can wreak havoc on your internal clock. Imagine this: You're engrossed in a thrilling plot twist, and suddenly, your stomach joins the suspense. "Is it the killer or just indigestion?" you wonder. Timing is crucial. Aim for a pre-movie pit stop, or risk missing the climax (of the film, that is).

Section 3: The Stealthy Stall Strategy
1. **The Bathroom Recon**: Upon arrival, scout the restroom situation. Is it a serene oasis or a chaotic vortex? Note the number of stalls, the quality of hand soap, and the ambient music level. If it's a single-stall affair, pray that your date doesn't need to go simultaneously. Awkwardness level: intergalactic.

2. **The Whispering Flush**: In the restroom, execute the whisper-flush technique. As you release the Kraken, gently press the lever. The goal? Minimal noise. You're not launching a rocket; you're maintaining the illusion of elegance. Bonus points if you hum a love ballad while flushing.

Section 4: The Post-Poop Playbook

1. **The Freshening Ritual**: Wash your hands thoroughly. Use soap, not just water. You're not a barbarian. Dry your hands with grace, as if preparing for a piano recital. Spritz a hint of cologne or perfume—subtle, like a secret shared between lovers.
2. **The Exit Strategy**: As you return to your date, act nonchalant. Engage in witty banter. Smile. Avoid phrases like, "You won't believe what just happened in there!" Instead, steer the conversation toward mutual interests. "Speaking of black holes, have you ever considered time travel?"

Conclusion

And there you have it, fellow daters. The secret to successful pooping on a date lies in timing, finesse, and a dash of cosmic humour. So go forth, embrace the unknown, and remember: Love is like a well-timed flush—it can either sweep you off your feet or leave you feeling flushed.

The Lavatory Companion

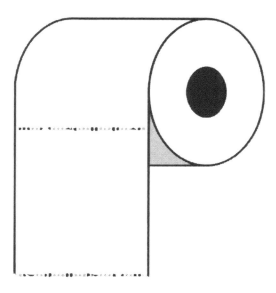

TOILET SMOKERS: A PUFF OF ABSURDITY

Introduction
In the quiet corridors of everyday life, where porcelain meets contemplation, there exists a peculiar subculture—the toilet smokers. These rebels of restroom etiquette defy convention, puffing away in the most unlikely of places. Buckle up, my friends, as we delve into this cloud of absurdity.

Section 1: The Lavatory Lounge
1. **The Secret Society**: Picture it—a dimly lit restroom, the air thick with anticipation. Our protagonist, a mild-mannered office worker, enters a stall. But wait! The adjacent stall emits a faint glow—a cigarette tip burning like a distant star. It's the initiation—the moment they become part of the clandestine Lavatory Lounge.
2. **The Whispered Exhale**: As our hero sits, they hear it—the soft exhale of a fellow toilet smoker. "Psst," comes the voice, "mind passing the lighter?" And there, beneath the partition, a hand extends—a nicotine communion in the most unlikely of sanctuaries.

Section 2: The Art of Disguise
1. **The Stealthy Stash**: Toilet smokers are masters of concealment. They hide lighters in soap dispensers, stash cigarettes behind toilet paper rolls, and camouflage ashtrays as air fresheners. The janitor, unsuspecting, empties the "scented" receptacle, unaware of the smoky secrets within.
2. **The Synchronized Puff**: Imagine a synchronized swimming routine, but with cigarettes. Two toilet smokers, puffing in harmony—one inhales, the other exhales. Their eyes meet above the stall dividers, a silent pact forged. It's a dance of nicotine and camaraderie.

Section 3: The Smoke Signals
1. **The Code of Rings**: Toilet smokers communicate through smoke rings. A single ring means "All clear." Double rings signal "Janitor approaching." And a triple ring? That's the emergency code—an unexpected visit from the boss. Our hero, mid-puff, extinguishes the evidence, praying their PowerPoint presentation remains unscathed.
2. **The Ashtray Etiquette**: When the ashtray fills, it's a delicate operation. Our protagonist balances the overflowing tray on one knee, taps the ashes into the toilet, and flushes—the ultimate

vanishing act. The janitor, unknowingly, disposes of the evidence. The cycle continues.

Section 4: The Exit Strategy
1. **The Final Drag**: As our hero leaves the restroom, they take one last drag—the taste of rebellion lingering. They adjust their tie, re-enter the office, and resume spreadsheet duties. No one suspects—the toilet smokers remain hidden, their secret safe within the porcelain walls.
2. **The Smoke-Free Elevator**: In the elevator, our protagonist stands next to the boss. The scent of mint gum masks the faint tobacco residue. The boss smiles, unaware. "Good morning," they say. Our hero nods, thinking, "And a good morning to you, fellow toilet smoker."

Conclusion
So, my friends, next time you visit the restroom, glance at the soap dispenser. Is it really soap, or a lighter in disguise? Remember—the Lavatory Lounge awaits, where smoke swirls and office politics fade.

The Lavatory Companion

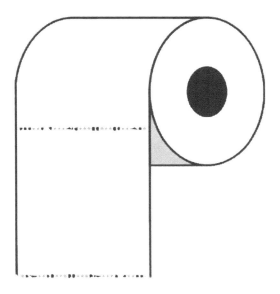

THE BRISTOL STOOL CHART: A JOURNEY THROUGH THE BOWEL GALAXY

Introduction

Ladies and gentlemen, fasten your seatbelts and secure your tray tables. We're about to embark on a cosmic adventure—one that takes us deep into the uncharted territory of our digestive universe. Welcome aboard the **Bristol Stool Chart Express!**

Section 1: Constellation Constipation

Picture this: you're in the bathroom, pondering life's mysteries while perched upon your porcelain throne. Suddenly, a celestial map appears before you—the **Bristol Stool Chart**. It's like the Milky Way of bowel movements, with seven distinct constellations:

1. **Type 1: The Rabbit Pellets**: These little nuggets resemble rabbit droppings. You're not pooping; you're launching mini meteorites. Perhaps you've been nibbling on cosmic carrots?
2. **Type 2: The Lumpy Constellation**: Like a distant asteroid belt, these stools are lumpy and hard. They require Herculean effort to escape Earth's gravitational pull. Remember, constipation is just a wormhole away.
3. **Type 3: The Sausage Link**: Ah, the classic sausage link—a cosmic delicacy. It's smooth, but not too smooth. Just like Goldilocks' porridge, it's juuust right. You're cruising through the asteroid belt with ease.

Section 2: The Black Hole of Despair

4. **Type 4: The Perfect Log**: Behold, the majestic space log! It's well-formed, like a rocket ready for launch. No turbulence here—just a smooth ride to the stars. You're officially in warp speed.
5. **Type 5: The Soft Serve Nebula**: Imagine a swirling nebula of soft-serve ice cream. These stools are fluffy, like marshmallow clouds. But beware—they can leave a sticky residue on your spaceship walls.
6. **Type 6: The Exploding Comet**: Brace yourself! These are liquid meteor showers. You're not just flushing; you're launching a cosmic explosion. Grab your helmet and hold on tight. Houston, we have a problem.
7. **Type 7: The Liquid Black Hole**: Congratulations, you've entered the event horizon. These black holes suck you in—no escape. It's like falling into a wormhole of doom. But fear not; you'll emerge on the

other side, slightly dehydrated and questioning your life choices.

Conclusion
Dear travellers, as we conclude our journey through the Bristol Stool Chart galaxy, remember this: every poop is a celestial event. Whether you're a shooting star or a distant quasar, embrace your cosmic uniqueness.

And may your flushes propel you toward new horizons—where no toilet has gone before!

THE ALTERNATIVE BRISTOL STOOL CHART

Drop Anchor

Depth Charge

Party Trick

Coiled Cobra

Bombs Away

Britains Got Bidets

LOO OF LEGENDS: PART V

The Enigma of the Phantom Flush

In the shadowy depths of the "Loo of Legends," where the tiles whispered secrets and the air hummed with anticipation, Sir Armitage encountered a perplexing phenomenon—the Phantom Flush. This spectral disturbance defied logic, plumbing, and common decency.

The Midnight Symphony
At precisely midnight, when the moon hung low and the bathroom tiles harmonized in a minor key, the toilet tank stirred. Its water sloshed, lids trembled, and the handle twitched. Sir Armitage clad in his plaid pyjamas, watched in awe.

"What sorcery is this?" he muttered, gripping his toothbrush like a sword.

The Haunting H2O
The Phantom Flush had no physical form, but its presence was palpable. It whispered through the pipes, *"Flush me, Armitage. Set me free."*

"Why dost thou haunt the porcelain?" Sir Armitage asked, his voice echoing off the tiles.

"Because," the Phantom Flush replied, *"I am the residue of forgotten wishes. Every unfulfilled dream, every abandoned resolution—it all collects here. I yearn for release."*

The Quest for Closure
Sir Armitage pondered. Should he heed the Phantom Flush's plea or dismiss it as nocturnal nonsense? The stakes were high—the fate of unflushed aspirations hung in the balance.

"Choose wisely," warned the bidet seat. *"For I control destiny—one spray at a time."*

The Final Flush
Sir Armitage took a deep breath, grasped the toilet handle, and closed his eyes. The tank gurgled, the water swirled, and the Phantom Flush let out a contented sigh.

"Thank you," it whispered. *"Now, go forth and pursue your dreams. And remember, Armitage sometimes life needs a good reset."*

Moral of the Story:
"In the realm of restrooms, even the ethereal seeks closure. Listen to the whispers, embrace the mysteries, and never underestimate the power of a well-timed flush."

And so, Sir Armitage left the Phantom Flush behind, its spectral ripples fading into the porcelain. As he exited, the tiles hummed a farewell tune, and the toilet paper dispenser dispenses his little jig.

The Lavatory Companion

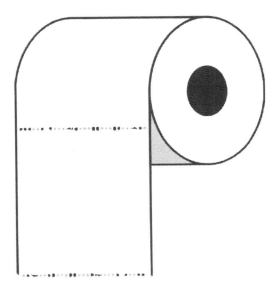

TALES FROM THE TAVERN: PUB TOILETS

Introduction
Ah, the pub toilet—a mysterious realm where ale-fuelled adventures meet porcelain practicality. Forget dragons and knights; here, the real quest is finding a clean seat. In this chapter, we raise our tankards to the unsung heroes—the pub toilets.

Section 1: The Drunken Labyrinth
Picture this: You stumble into a dimly lit pub, the air thick with laughter and the scent of spilled beer. The pub toilet awaits—a beacon of relief in a sea of inebriation. But beware! The path is treacherous:
1. **The Broken Lock**: The door swings open, revealing a broken lock. You balance on one leg, guarding the entrance like a tipsy sentry.
2. **The Graffiti Gallery**: Inside, the walls tell tales of love, loss, and questionable spelling. "For a good time, call Ethel" is scrawled next to a phone number that's missing a digit.
3. **The Mystery Stain**: You eye the floor. Is it beer? Blood? Or something more sinister? You tiptoe around it, muttering a silent prayer to the cleaning gods.

Section 2: The Soap Opera
In the pub toilet, drama unfolds:
1. **The Soap Dispenser Saga**: You pump the soap dispenser. Nothing. You pump again. Still nothing. You contemplate using beer as a makeshift sanitizer.
2. **The Hand Dryer Dilemma**: The hand dryer roars to life, threatening to blow your skin off. You opt for the classic pants wipe.
3. **The Mirror Monologue**: You gaze into the mirror. Your reflection wavers, a blurry hero with beer foam in your Mustache. You deliver a motivational speech to your bleary-eyed twin.

Conclusion
As you stumble back to the bar, raise your tankard. To the pub toilets—the unsung heroes who absorb spilled secrets, witness drunken confessions, and keep the ale-soaked world turning.

And remember, fellow travellers: When in doubt, always tip the restroom attendant. They've seen things.

The Lavatory Companion

The Lavatory Companion

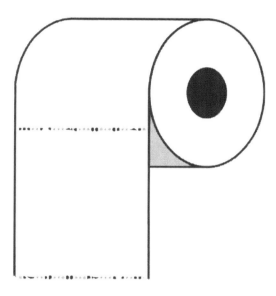

THE CAMPER VAN COMMODE: SLIPPERY ROADS AHEAD

Introduction
Ah, the open road—the wind in your hair, the freedom to explore, and the sudden realization that you really need to go. Welcome to the Camper Van Commode Chronicles, where we delve into the delicate art of doing your business on four wheels.

Section 1: The Nomadic Necessity
Picture this: You're parked by a serene lakeside, the sun setting in hues of orange and gold. The world is your oyster, and your camper van is your trusty steed. But nature calls, and the nearest restroom is miles away. Fear not! Your van holds the key to liberation.
1. **The Portable Throne**: Behold, your portable throne—a compact commode that transforms your van into a private lavatory. It's like having a VIP pass to the loo, wherever you roam.
2. **The Stealth Stop**: You pull over on a deserted country road, curtains drawn. The world outside remains blissfully unaware as you embark on your mission. Remember, discretion is key.

Section 2: The Art of Camper Van Squatting
1. **The Contortionist Stance**: Space is limited, so you assume the contortionist stance—a delicate balance between crouching and hovering. Your yoga teacher would be proud.
2. **The Window View**: Some camper vans boast scenic windows strategically positioned near the toilet. As you squat, you gaze out at rolling hills or a quaint village. It's like a moving postcard.
3. **The Toilet Paper Tango**: You reach for the roll, only to discover it's rolled off the holder during your last turn. No worries! You perform the Toilet Paper Tango—a graceful pirouette to retrieve it from the floor.

Section 3: The Grey Water Ballet
1. **The Grey Water Dilemma**: After your performance, it's time for the encore—the grey water disposal. You tiptoe to the designated drain, hose in hand. It's a delicate ballet of emptying tanks without splashing your shoes.
2. **The Stealthy Exit**: You slip back into the driver's seat, your secret safe. The van purrs to life, and you drive away, leaving no trace of

your artistic endeavours.

Conclusion

As you continue your nomadic journey, remember: The Camper Van Commode Chronicles are a testament to resourcefulness, adaptability, and the sheer audacity of doing your business with a view. So, raise your travel mug to the open road—and may your grey water always flow downstream.

The Lavatory Companion

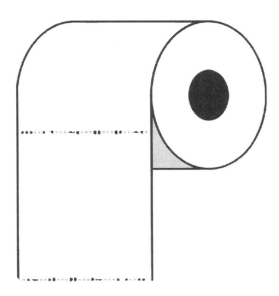

THE COVERT PLUMBERS HANDBOOK

Introduction
In the shadowy world of clandestine toilet activities, discretion is key. Whether you're rerouting sewage, installing secret bidets, or conducting advanced underwater plumbing experiments, you must avoid detection at all costs. Fear not, dear reader, for this handbook shall equip you with the tools and tactics necessary to outwit even the most seasoned plumber.

Chapter 1: The Art of Subterfuge
1. **Choose Your Cover Story Wisely**:
    - When the plumber arrives, act casual. Mention a minor leak or a faulty flush mechanism. Avoid phrases like "I've been tinkering with the pipes" or "I'm a self-taught bidet engineer."
    - If questioned, claim you're an amateur plumber enthusiast. Say you've been binge-watching plumbing tutorials on YouTube. Bonus points if you can name-drop a famous plumber vlogger.
2. **Strategic Distractions**:
    - Keep a stack of plumbing magazines near the toilet. When the plumber enters, casually flip through them. Mutter phrases like "Ah, yes, the intricacies of U-bends" or "Fascinating ballcock mechanisms."
    - Hang a poster of Mario (from Super Mario Bros.) in the bathroom. If the plumber raises an eyebrow, say it's your "inspiration wall."

Chapter 2: Concealment Techniques
1. **The Chalkboard Ruse**:
    - Scribble complex equations on the bathroom chalkboard. When the plumber asks, explain that you're solving the mysteries of quantum plumbing. Use terms like "flux capacitor" and "toilet singularity."
2. **The Rubber Glove Alibi**:
    - Hang rubber gloves conspicuously. When questioned, say you're practicing safe hygiene. If pressed further, claim you're preparing for a "toilet archaeology expedition."

Chapter 3: Advanced Tactics
1. **The Distracting Soundtrack**:
    - Play recordings of soothing ocean waves or whale songs. When the plumber furrows their brow, say it helps you focus on pipe alignment.
    - If caught, switch to a playlist of classic plumber anthems: "I Will Survive" and "Drain It Like It's Hot."
2. **The Emergency Drill**:
    - Rig a fake emergency button near the toilet. When the plumber investigates, dramatically press it. Flashing lights and sirens should distract them.
    - Explain it's your "plumbing panic button" for dire situations.

Chapter 4: Exit Strategies
1. **The Emergency Phone Call**:
    - Have a friend call you during the plumber's visit. Answer loudly, "Yes, the secret bidet prototype is ready for deployment!" Hang up abruptly.
    - Apologize to the plumber, blaming it on your "plumbing think tank."
2. **The Vanishing Act**:
    - When the plumber isn't looking, slip into the bathroom cabinet. Pretend you've vanished. Reappear later, dishevelled, and say, "I was inspecting the u-bend from within."

Conclusion
Remember, dear reader, the path of the covert plumber is treacherous. But with cunning, creativity, and a plunger in hand, you can protect your clandestine plumbing legacy. May your bidets remain hidden, your leaks discreet, and your secrets safely flushed away.

The Lavatory Companion

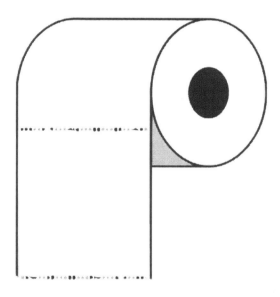

THE UNSPOKEN TRUTHS OF TOILET OWNERSHIP

Introduction: Congratulations, dear reader! You are now the proud owner of a porcelain throne—a gateway to both relief and revelation. But beware, for the toilet owner's manual conveniently omits certain crucial details. Fear not, for we shall unveil the clandestine hilarities that await you in the world of lavatories.

Section 1: The Art of Seat Negotiation
1. **The Hover Technique**:
    - The manual says: "Sit comfortably." But reality? We've all perfected the hover—balancing precariously above the seat like a gymnast on a pommel horse. Why? Because public restrooms are a microbial minefield, and our glutes are the last line of defence.
2. **The Stealth Flush**:
    - Ever flushed mid-business to mask embarrassing sounds? It's an art form. The manual should include a chapter titled "Flush Like a Ninja: Silent, Swift, and Shame-Proof."

Section 2: The Toilet Paper Chronicles
1. **The Endless Roll Mystery**:
    - Why does the roll vanish faster than a magician's rabbit? The manual should reveal the truth: Toilet paper is a sentient being with a penchant for escape. It unspools itself when you're not looking.
2. **The One-Ply Dilemma**:
    - The manual suggests frugality. But one-ply? It's like wiping with tracing paper. We deserve better. Let's unite for fluffier futures!

Section 3: The Phantom Flush Phenomenon
1. **The Ghostly Flush**:
    - You're alone, minding your business, when suddenly—the toilet flushes. No one's there. Is it a spectral janitor? A plumbing poltergeist? The manual should clarify: "Your toilet has a secret admirer. Accept it."
2. **The Post-Flush Symphony**:
    - The manual claims silence post-flush. But no! The pipes

erupt in a cacophony—a waterlogged opera. It's the toilet's way of saying, "Bravo! Encore!"

Section 4: The Toilet Seat Conspiracy
1. **The Seat Position Wars**:
    - The manual avoids this topic. But we know the truth: The seat has three positions—up, down, and "hovered." Each sparks marital debates, roommate feuds, and existential crises.
2. **The Midnight Encounter**:
    - You stumble half-asleep into the bathroom, only to plunge into icy water. The seat was left up. The manual should warn: "Toilet seats are shape-shifters. Always check."

Section 5: The Toilet Door Etiquette
1. **The Awkward Exit**:
    - You emerge from the stall, and there they are—the next person waiting. Eye contact? Forbidden. The manual should advise: "Exit briskly, like a secret agent escaping a compromised mission."
2. **The Stall Selection Strategy**:
    - The manual says nothing about stall hierarchy. But we know: The middle stall is the Goldilocks zone—neither too close nor too far. The end stalls? Reserved for rebels and introverts.

Conclusion
Remember, dear reader, the toilet is more than porcelain and pipes. It's a theatre of absurdity, a confessional booth, and a place where humanity reveals its quirks. So, embrace the hilarity, keep your plunger handy, and may your toilet tales be as epic as the Odyssey (with fewer sea monsters).

The Lavatory Companion

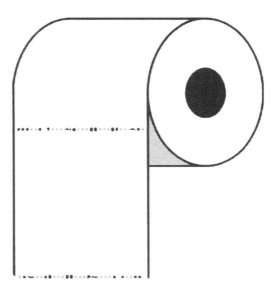

LOO OF LEGENDS: PART VI

Flushed with Love

In the dimly lit restroom of the "Loo of Legends," where the tiles whispered secrets and the air crackled with romantic tension, Sir Armitage stumbled upon a love story—a tale woven between the porcelain stalls.

The Cubicle Conundrum
As Sir Armitage adjusted his plaid pyjamas and contemplated the mysteries of life, he heard a soft voice from the last cubicle. *"Psst! Sir Armitage!"* it whispered. *"I'm stuck."*

He tiptoed toward the cubicle, where the door was jammed. And there, amidst the toilet paper rolls and graffiti, stood Lady Isabella—a vision in mismatched socks and dishevelled hair.

The Toilet Paper Serenade
"Lady Isabella," Sir Armitage said, his heart doing a waltz. *"Why dost thou linger in this confined space?"*

She blushed, her cheeks rivalling the pink soap dispenser. *"I sought refuge from the world,"* she confessed. *"And now I'm trapped. The door mocks me, like an unsent love letter."

"Fear not," Sir Armitage declared. *"I shall free thee. But first, a serenade."*
And so, he sang—a ballad of bidets, hand dryers, and shared hand sanitizer. Lady Isabella's eyes sparkled, and the toilet paper dispenser hummed along.

The Great Escape
Sir Armitage jimmied the door, his plunger acting as a makeshift lever. With a triumphant flush, the cubicle released Lady Isabella. She stepped out, her smile brighter than the fluorescent lights.

"Thou art my hero," she said, her hand brushing against his. *"And this restroom, our secret garden."

The Toilet Paper Confession
As they exited the cubicle, hand in hand, Lady Isabella whispered, *"Sir Armitage I have a confession. I wrote the cryptic graffiti—the one about Elvis and the bidet."*

He chuckled. *"And I,"* he confessed, *"am the Phantom Flush."
"Together," she said, *"we shall rewrite the bathroom code. No more unsent love letters. Just shared hand sanitizer and whispered promises."

Moral of the Story:
"In the realm of restrooms, love blooms in unexpected corners. Embrace the quirks, dance with the toilet paper, and remember that sometimes, the best connections happen when you're stuck."

And so, Sir Armitage and Lady Isabella left the Loo of Legends, their hearts flushed with hope. As they exited, the tiles hummed a love song, and the air freshener released a burst of "Romantic Rose."

The Lavatory Companion

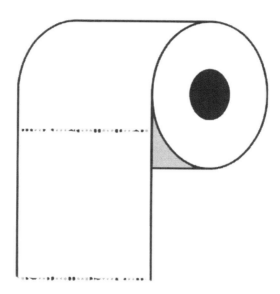

THE QUEST OF ADVANCED WIPING SOLUTIONS

Introduction: As the world spins on its porcelain axis, let us explore uncharted territories—the wild and wacky alternatives to traditional toilet paper. For when the TP shelf is bare, fear not! These hilarious options await your adventurous derrière.

Section 1: The Bidet Ballet
1. **The Bidet Symphony**:
    - Bidets, those elegant water fountains for your nether regions, deserve a standing ovation. Picture this: a gentle stream of aqua caressing your bum like a spa massage. Bonus points if it plays Vivaldi's "Four Seasons" during the rinse.
2. **The Bidet Duel**:
    - Invite a friend over, each armed with a bidet. Engage in a water-spraying showdown. The last one dry wins. Loser gets a soggy high-five.

Section 2: Leaves of Legend
1. **Mullein Leaves**:
    - Wander into the woods, find a mullein plant, and pluck its velvety leaves. Soft, absorbent, and eco-friendly. Just beware of forest critters critiquing your technique.
2. **Banana Leaves**:
    - Nature's gift to your behind. Grab a banana leaf, wipe with flair, and channel your inner Tarzan. Bonus: It doubles as a tropical fan.

Section 3: Paper Products Reimagined
1. **Facial Tissue Fandango**:
    - Raid the tissue box. Unfold a delicate tissue square, hold it aloft, and declare, "I am the monarch of my bathroom!" Then dab daintily.
2. **Paper Towel Tango**:
    - In moments of desperation, reach for the kitchen roll. Its rugged texture exfoliates while it absorbs. Warning: May leave you feeling like a lumberjack.

Section 4: The Art of Repurposing

1. **Receipt Rendezvous**:
    - That crumpled receipt from last week's grocery run? It's your emergency TP. Read it aloud for added entertainment. "Item 1: Kale. Item 2: Regret."
2. **Coffee Filter Chronicles**:
    - Unleash your inner barista. Grab a coffee filter, pretend it's a delicate pour-over, and filter out life's messiest moments.

Section 5: The Grand Finale
1. **The Curtain Call**:
    - Gather your audience (household members, pets, imaginary friends). Unroll a roll of bubble wrap. Pop each bubble with flair. Declare, "Behold, the sound of cleanliness!"
2. **The TP Time Capsule**:
    - Bury a roll of toilet paper in your backyard. Label it "2024: The Great Shortage." Dig it up in 50 years. Imagine the confusion of future archaeologists.

Conclusion
Remember, dear reader, life's quirkiest moments happen in the bathroom. So, embrace the absurdity, experiment with these alternatives, and may your wiping adventures be legendary!

The Lavatory Companion

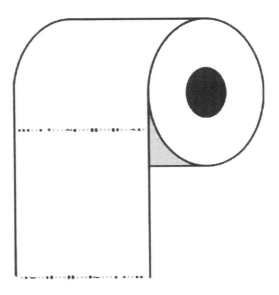

THE ART OF POOP DISPOSAL: A DESPERATE DILEMMA

Introduction
Ah, the dreaded moment when your porcelain chariot fails you—the toilet refuses to swallow your offerings. Fear not, fellow faecal voyager! In this chapter, we delve into the clandestine world of poop concealment when the flush falters.

Section 1: The Emergency Toolkit
1. **The Toilet Paper Mummy**:
    - Grab the nearest roll of toilet paper. Swaddle your creation like a newborn—layer upon layer. Tuck it into the trash bin, whispering, "Rest in peace, my little friend."
2. **The Tissue Burial Ground**:
    - Unroll an entire box of facial tissues. Bury your shame beneath the fluffy white layers. Bonus points if you hum a funeral dirge.

Section 2: The Creative Camouflage
1. **The Dirty Laundry Diversion**:
    - Open the laundry hamper. Nestle your unflushable treasure among the socks and undies. When questioned, blame it on the dog. Or the cat. Or the invisible sock monster.
2. **The Potted Plant Ploy**:
    - Locate a houseplant. Dig a small hole in its soil. Deposit your payload. Cover it with care. Water the plant, whispering, "May your leaves thrive on my secret."

Section 3: The DIY Plumbing Magic
1. **The Hanger Hook Trick**:
    - Unravel a wire hanger. Shape it into a hook. Fish out your stubborn stowaway. Wave it like a trophy. Declare, "Behold, the excrement exorcised!"
2. **The Hot Water Ritual**:
    - Boil a kettle. Pour hot water into the bowl. Whisper incantations like, "By the power of steam, I banish thee!" Pray the porcelain gods are merciful.

Section 4: The Stealthy Exit Strategy

1. **The Nonchalant Nudge**:
    - Casually sidle out of the bathroom. Find the homeowner. Say, "Lovely place you've got here. By the way, your toilet is... quirky. Any tips?"
2. **The Distraction Dance**:
    - Burst into the living room. Announce, "Guess what? I can moonwalk!" Execute a flawless moonwalk. When they're sufficiently baffled, slip back to the bathroom.

Section 5: The Final Frontier
1. **The Time Capsule Commode**:
    - Wrap your unflushable relic in aluminium foil. Bury it in the backyard. Mark the spot with a tiny flag. Inscribe, "Here lies my dignity. Handle with care."
2. **The Cosmic Flush Conspiracy**:
    - Stare at the toilet. Whisper, "Maybe it's not broken. Maybe it's an interdimensional portal. My poop is now exploring parallel universes." Flush dramatically.

Conclusion
Remember, dear reader, desperate times call for desperate measures. May your unflushable escapades remain legendary, and may your bathroom tales be whispered in hushed tones across generations.

The Lavatory Companion

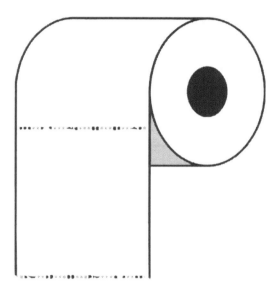

THAT SINKING FEELING: WHEN DESPERATION STRIKES

Introduction
Life is a series of unexpected twists, and sometimes, the porcelain gods conspire against us. When the toilet refuses its duty, and you're left with a pressing matter, fear not! This chapter explores the clandestine art of sink-based defecation—a desperate dance between hygiene and humiliation.

Section 1: The Sink Selection Process
1. **The Sink Survey**:
   - Assess your options. Is it a sleek bathroom vanity sink or a rustic farmhouse basin? Consider aesthetics, depth, and splash potential. Remember, this choice will shape your legacy.
2. **The Faucet Factor**:
   - A high-arc faucet provides more clearance. A low-profile one? Risky business. Imagine the headlines: "Local Resident Wedged in Bathroom Sink—Film at Eleven."

Section 2: The Stealthy Setup
1. **The Towel Tourniquet**:
   - Drape a bath towel over your shoulders like a cape. Declare, "I am the Sink Avenger!" Proceed with pooping prowess.
2. **The Soap Opera**:
   - Lather your hands with soap. Pretend it's a sacred ritual. Whisper, "May the porcelain gods forgive me." Then assume the position.

Section 3: The Art of Execution
1. **The Squat Symphony**:
   - Balance on the sink's edge. Assume a yogic squat. Channel your inner Cirque du Soleil performer. Bonus points for maintaining eye contact with your reflection.
2. **The Stealth Splashdown**:
   - Release your payload. Aim for the drain. Pray the sink's plumbing can handle this unexpected detour. Whisper, "May the pipes be merciful."

Section 4: The Cleanup Conundrum

1. **The Handwashing Hurdle**:
     o   Rinse your hands. Contemplate your life choices. Wonder if this is how astronauts feel in zero gravity. Sing "Happy Birthday" twice for good measure.
2. **The Towel Dilemma**:
     o   Dry your hands. Realize the towel now bears witness to your sink-based saga. Fold it neatly. Hang it back. Pretend nothing happened.

Section 5: The Exit Strategy
1. **The Nonchalant Return**:
     o   Rejoin the party. Smile mysteriously. When someone asks, "Where were you?" reply, "Oh, just exploring new dimensions." Leave them bewildered.
2. **The Sink Souvenir**:
     o   Snap a selfie with the sink. Caption it, "Sink Chronicles: Chapter 11." Share it on social media. Await the flood of confused emojis.

Conclusion
And so, dear sink-based defecators, may your porcelain quests be ever daring, your plungers ever heroic, and your aquatic escapades forever etched in bathroom folklore.

Remember: Life's greatest adventures often involve sinks, seagulls, and unexpected flotsam. May your plunges be precise, your faucets forgiving, and your turds—well, may they float on.

The Lavatory Companion

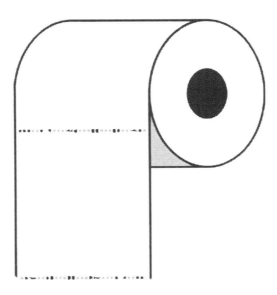

THE HOLE-IN-THE-FLOOR: A DANCE WITH DESTINY

Introduction: In the annals of bathroom history, few designs evoke both fascination and trepidation like the hole-in-the-floor latrine. Whether you encounter it in a remote village or a quirky café, this chapter explores the delicate art of balancing over an abyss—a waltz with destiny, if you will.

Section 1: The Architectural Ballet
1. **The Grand Entrance:**
    - Picture it: You step into a dimly lit room. The air smells of ancient secrets and disinfectant. There, in the centre, lies the hole—a dark chasm that defies gravity and reason. You take a deep breath. It's showtime.
2. **The Stance of Contemplation:**
    - Survey the scene. The hole gapes like a hungry mouth. Your feet straddle the precipice. You ponder life's mysteries: "Why am I here? What did I eat for lunch?"

Section 2: The Graviton
1. **The Squat Symphony:**
    - Lower yourself gracefully. Imagine you're auditioning for a modern dance troupe. Flexibility is key. Ignore the spider in the corner; it's your silent partner.
2. **The Balance Beam Waltz:**
    - Extend your arms. Find equilibrium. Whisper, "I am one with the void." Ignore the cold tiles against your skin. They're merely the orchestra's percussion section.

Section 3: The Splashdown Pas de Deux
1. **The Precise Release:**
    - Time your descent. Too soon, and you risk disaster. Too late, and—well, let's not think about that. Aim for the bullseye. Channel your inner archer.
2. **The Echoing Sump:**
    - Listen. The splash echoes like applause. You've performed admirably. Wipe with leaves or imagination. Rise like a phoenix from the abyss.

Section 4: The Exit Curtain Call

1. **The Stealthy Retreat**:
    - Exit with grace. Avoid eye contact with fellow patrons. They know. They always know. Wash your hands. Whisper, "Farewell, hole. Until we meet again."
2. **The Post-Performance Reflection**:
    - Look in the mirror. Your eyes say, "I survived." Your soul says, "I have a story to tell." Embrace it. Share it. And remember: Life is a dance, and sometimes, you pirouette over a hole in the floor.

Conclusion

Remember, dear reader, the hole-in-the-floor latrine is more than a restroom—it's a stage. So, embrace the choreography, tip your imaginary hat to the audience, and may your bathroom tales be etched in the annals of absurdity.

The Lavatory Companion

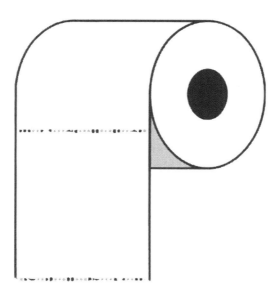

LOO OF LEGENDS: PART VII

Bristles of Betrayal

In the dimly lit restroom of the "Loo of Legends," where the tiles whispered secrets and the air crackled with ancient vendettas, Sir Armitage faced an old foe—the **Toilet Brush**. This bristled adversary had haunted his bathroom adventures for years, and now, fate had brought them together once more.

The Bristled Reunion
As Sir Armitage adjusted his plaid pyjamas, he noticed the toilet brush leaning against the sink. Its bristles twitched, and its handle bore battle scars from countless scrubbing sessions.

"Ah, Armitage" it hissed. *"We meet again."*

The Brush's Grudge
The toilet brush had a score to settle. It remembered every swipe, every splash, and every indignant flush. It had witnessed Sir Armitage's clumsiness—the toothpaste splatters, the soap spills, and the occasional hairball fiasco.

"You think you can escape your messes?" the brush spat. *"I am the keeper of cleanliness, the scourge of scum. Prepare for a bristled reckoning!"*

The Duel of Suds
Sir Armitage squared his shoulders. He had faced dragons, phantom flushes, and even the bidet uprising. But the toilet brush was a different beast—a relentless cleaner with a grudge.

"Very well," he declared. *"Let us duel, old friend."*

And so, they battled—a clash of porcelain and nylon. The brush lunged, scrubbing furiously. Sir Armitage dodged, sidestepping suds and avoiding the dreaded toilet rim.

The Sudsy Truce
As the dust settled (or rather, the soap scum), Sir Armitage and the toilet brush locked eyes. Both were weary, both were splattered, and both had newfound respect for each other's tenacity.

"Why dost thou persist?" Sir Armitage asked, wiping a sudsy streak from his cheek.

"Because," the brush replied, *"*"cleanliness is my purpose. And you, Armitage are my eternal challenge."

Moral of the Story:
"In the realm of restrooms, foes can become allies. Embrace the bristles, learn from the splashes, and remember that even the lowliest brush has a story to scrub."

And so, Sir Armitage left the toilet brush by the sink, its bristles drooping in exhaustion. As he exited, the tiles hummed a soapy farewell, and the air freshener released a burst of "Lemon Zest."

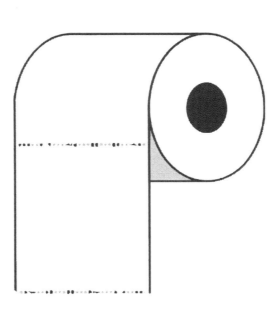

WILDERNESS WOES: OUTOOR LOGGING

Introduction
Ah, the great outdoors—the cathedral of nature, where leaves rustle, birds sing, and the call of the wild beckons. But when your bowels stage a coup, and civilization is miles away, you face the ultimate test: how to have a dignified dump in the woods. Fear not, fellow wanderer; this chapter is your guide to sylvan sanitation.

Section 1: The Art of Spot Selection
1. **The Sacred Distance**:
    - Wander at least **200 feet** from any trail, campsite, or water source. This isn't a sprint; it's a pilgrimage. Find a secluded spot where the trees nod in approval.
2. **The Perfect Perch**:
    - Survey your surroundings. Choose a fallen log, a mossy rock, or a friendly stump. Avoid ant hills, poison ivy, and nettles—unless you're into that sort of adventure.

Section 2: The Squat Symphony
1. **The Zen Squat**:
    - Assume the position: feet shoulder-width apart, knees slightly bent. Channel your inner woodland creature. Whisper, "I am one with the forest."
2. **The Leafy Lament**:
    - Grab a handful of leaves. Not too spiky, not too slimy. Imagine they're your eco-friendly toilet paper. Bonus points if they're maple leaves—the Rolls-Royce of foliage.

Section 3: The Earthy Embrace
1. **The Digging Dance**:
    - Grab a sturdy stick. Dig a **6–8-inch hole** in the soft earth. Pretend you're unearthing buried treasure. If you find actual treasure, please share.
2. **The Poop Ritual**:
    - Release your burden. Marvel at the simplicity of it all. Whisper, "Thank you, Mother Nature." Cover your creation with soil. Pat it down like a proud gardener.

Section 4: The Hygienic Hymn
1. **The Handwashing Overture**:
   - Use water if available. If not, rub your hands with dirt. It's like a natural exfoliant. Sing a woodland ballad while you scrub.
2. **The Leave-No-Trace Finale**:
   - Pack out used toilet paper in a sealed bag. Or better yet, use biodegradable wipes. Leave the forest as pristine as you found it. The trees will nod in gratitude.

Conclusion
Remember, dear reader, the woods are our sanctuary. Treat them kindly, and they'll cradle your secrets. May your wilderness poops be harmonious, your leaves abundant, and your adventures—well, wild.

The Lavatory Companion

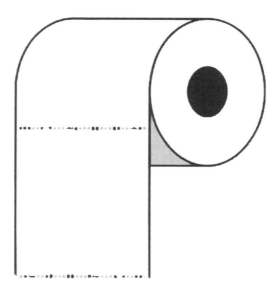

THE MISADVENTURES OF THE WAYWARD POO

Introduction
In the grand theatre of life, there exists a tragicomic act—one that transcends embarrassment and enters the realm of slapstick. Picture this: You're perched on the porcelain throne, aiming for glory, when fate intervenes. Your aim falters, and your precious payload takes an unexpected detour. Welcome to the calamity of missing the toilet while pooping!

Section 1: The Fateful Release
1. **The Initial Confidence**:
   - You settle in, ready for business. The world narrows down to that crucial moment. Your sphincter whispers, "This is it, champ." You nod solemnly.
2. **The Sudden Shift**:
   - But wait! A sneeze, a creaky floorboard, or a rogue thought about pizza distracts you. Your aim wavers. The payload veers off course. Panic sets in.

Section 2: The Splashdown Spectacle
1. **The Gravity Tango**:
   - Your wayward creation splashes into uncharted waters—the cold, unforgiving bathroom floor. It's like a cannonball at a pool party, but with less applause.
2. **The Desperate Cleanup**:
   - You assess the damage. The floor bears witness to your misjudgement. You grab toilet paper, mop, or a sock (hey, improvisation is key) and mutter, "May this stain be forgotten."

Section 3: The Stealthy Exit
1. **The Walk of Shame**:
   - You emerge, face flushed (pun intended). Fellow bathroom-goers glance, eyebrows raised. You avoid eye contact. Your secret is safe—until they smell it.
2. **The Alibi**:
   - "Oh, that? Just testing the gravitational pull," you say, wiping your brow. "Science experiment. Very hush-hush."

Conclusion
Remember, dear reader, life's mishaps are the spice that seasons our existence. So, embrace the absurdity, aim true next time, and may your bathroom escapades be legendary—even if they involve a wayward poo.

MACRO, SOFT AND WINDOWS: AN ESCAPE STRATEGY

Introduction
In the annals of bathroom history, there exists a calamity so absurd, it defies all decorum—the desperate act of fleeing the toilet via the window. Picture it: You're mid-business, the porcelain thrones your witness, when disaster strikes. The flush fails, the door jams, and your dignity hangs by a thread. Fear not, dear reader; this chapter chronicles the art of the window escape—a tale of shame, agility, and questionable life choices.

Section 1: The Desperate Dilemma
1. **The Failed Flush**:
    - You've done your business. The toilet mocks you—a stagnant pool of regret. The handle refuses to budge. Panic sets in. The window beckons.
2. **The Window of Opportunity**:
    - You assess the situation. The window is small, the sill dusty. Outside, the world awaits—judgmental trees, curious squirrels, and perhaps a nosy neighbour with binoculars.

Section 2: The Stealthy Climb
1. **The Stealth Mode**:
    - You tiptoe, pants around your ankles. The window frame groans. You glance back at the toilet, whispering, "Forgive me." The porcelain remains stoic.
2. **The Spiderman Shuffle**:
    - One leg out, then the other. You straddle the sill, praying your balance holds. The breeze kisses your cheeks. You're halfway to freedom.

Section 3: The Graceful Exit
1. **The Leap of Faith**:
    - You hesitate. The ground is farther than it looked. But dignity demands sacrifice. You close your eyes and jump. The grass cushions your fall.
2. **The Walk of Shame Redux**:
    - You dust off your pants, survey the scene. The window remains open—a silent witness. You nod, vowing never to

return. The neighbour waves. You wave back.

Conclusion
Remember, dear reader, life's exits are rarely elegant. So, embrace the absurdity, keep your windows accessible, and may your escapes be swift—even if they involve a plunge into the unknown.

The Lavatory Companion

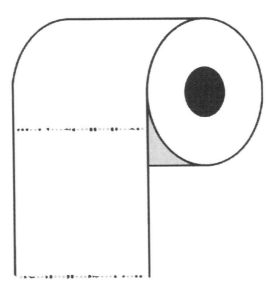

LOO OF LEGENDS: PART VIII

The Great Toilet Flood

In the hallowed halls of the "Loo of Legends," where the tiles whispered secrets and the air crackled with anticipation, Sir Armitage faced his most watery quest—the **Great Toilet Flood**. This was no ordinary leak; it was a deluge of epic proportions.

The Dripping Omen

Sir Armitage entered the restroom, his plaid pyjamas clinging to his ankles like damp seaweed. The air smelled of mildew, and the toilet paper dispenser hummed a mournful tune. But it was the ominous dripping sound that caught his attention—a rhythmic beat like a leaky faucet composing a symphony.

"Why dost thou weep, O porcelain vessel?" he asked, gazing at the toilet bowl.

The Rising Tide

The water level rose—an inch, then two. Sir Armitage's boots grew soggy, and the bidet seat blinked in alarm. The toilet brush, usually stoic, quivered in its corner.

"It's happening," whispered the brush. *"The prophecy foretold a flood—a cleansing baptism of chaos."

The Plunger's Call

Sir Armitage surveyed the scene. The water lapped at his ankles, and the toilet paper floated like tiny boats. He needed a hero—a saviour with rubbery resolve.
"Fetch the plunger!" he shouted to the janitor, who appeared with a mop and a knowing nod.

The Flushgate

And so, with a mighty plunge, Sir Armitage battled the rising tide. Water splashed, tiles trembled, and the toilet paper dispenser cheered.

"Fear not," he declared. *"We shall prevail!"

Moral of the Story:

"In the realm of restrooms, leaks happen. Embrace the soggy socks, laugh at the absurdity, and remember that sometimes, chaos leads to a clean slate."

And so, Sir Armitage left the flooded cubicle, his plaid pyjamas a little heavier. As he exited, the tiles hummed a farewell tune, and the air freshener released a burst of "Ocean Breeze."

And thus ends our watery saga—a tale of toilet floods, soggy quests, and the eternal quest for a dry exit. For now…

The Lavatory Companion

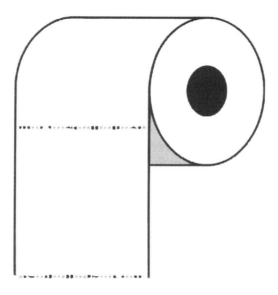

A BIRD IN THE HAND: THE EMU TECHNIQUE

Introduction
In the triple-ply scrolls of bathroom wisdom, where porcelain meets panic, there exists a chapter so absurd, it defies all plumbing logic—the legendary "Emu Technique." Picture it: You're trapped in a bathroom standoff, the toilet mocking you with its stubborn clog. The plunger is MIA, and your dignity hangs by a thread. Fear not, dear reader; as we embark on this dastardly deed involving a bin liner, gaffer tape, and a splash of insanity.

Section 1: The Emu Technique
1. **The Bin Liner Revelation**:
    - Gather your supplies: a bin liner (preferably unscented, for the sake of dignity), gaffer tape (the hero of our tale), and a steely resolve.
2. **The Arm Enrobing Ceremony**:
    - Roll up your sleeve. Channel your inner puppeteer. Slip your arm into the bin liner – all the way to the shoulder - sealing it like a medieval gauntlet. Secure with gaffer tape. Voilà! Your Emu Arm is ready. Wish the emu luck as it turns its head at you in disgust.

Section 2: The Toilet Test
1. **The Water-Tight Overture**:
    - Approach the toilet with gravitas. Your Emu Arm is your weapon. Insert it into the bowl, beak first. The water swirls, intrigued. The gaffer tape squeaks (or maybe that's just your nerves). Embody the graceful emu as it prepares for a plunge into a grassy nook - foraging for wormy morsels.
2. **The Desperate Plunge**:
    - Thrust your Emu Arm downward. Swirl, twist, and pirouette. Pretend you're in a waterlogged hand-ballet. The clog trembles (or maybe it's just the bin liner sweating). Use your beaked-companion to "shake hands" with the stool, and commence a deep stool massage.

Section 3: The Grand Flush Finale
1. **The Battle Cry**:
    - Yell, "For cleanliness! For sanity! For the love of all things

flushable!" The toilet clog quivers (perhaps seeking the spirit of Rod Hull for forgiveness).
2. **The Flush of Destiny**:
    o   Push the lever. The toilet roars—a cyclone of water, bin liner, and existential dread. Victory! The clog spirals away, defeated. The Emu Arm emerges, soggy, sad, but triumphant.

Conclusion

Remember, dear reader, when plungers fail, creativity prevails. So next time you face a toilet crisis, channel your inner Emu, tape up that bin liner, and may your bathroom escapades be legendary—even if they involve an arm-clad plunge.

The Lavatory Companion

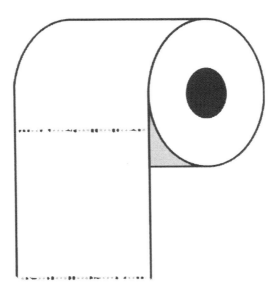

CUBICLE CRISIS: MISSING UNDERPANTS

Introduction
In the shadowy realm of bathroom mishaps, where porcelain meets perplexity, there exists a chapter so absurd, it could rival a magician's greatest trick—the legendary "Underpants Vanishing Act." Picture it: You're in the loo, minding your own business, when suddenly, your underpants decide to pull a Houdini. Fear not, dear reader; we delve into the world of disappearing briefs, cosmic vortexes, and a dash of embarrassment.

Section 1: The Underpants Portal
1. **The Bathroom Twilight Zone**:
    - Our unsuspecting hero, let's call them Captain Briefs, enters the bathroom. The air hums with anticipation. Captain Briefs disrobes, ready for the sacred ritual. But wait! Their underpants slip from their grasp, fluttering like startled butterflies. The cosmic portal opens.
2. **The Quantum Underpants Paradox**:
    - Captain Briefs watches in horror as their underpants defy gravity. They hover, then vanish into the void. Is it a black hole? A Bermuda Triangle for briefs? Captain Briefs contemplates existence.

Section 2: The Desperate Cover-Up
1. **The Toilet Paper Cape**:
    - Captain Briefs assesses the situation. They can't leave the bathroom half-naked. So, they grab a roll of toilet paper, wrap it around their waist, and declare, "I am the Toilet Paper Avenger!"
2. **The Stealthy Exit**:
    - Captain Briefs tiptoes out, toilet paper fluttering. Fellow bathroom-goers raise an eyebrow. Captain Briefs winks, whispering, "Fashion statement. Very avant-garde."

Section 3: The Grand Reveal
1. **The Laundry Quest**:
    - Captain Briefs embarks on a quest for fresh underpants. They raid drawers, laundry baskets, and forgotten gym bags. Alas, only mismatched socks and ancient boxers await.

2. **The Underpants Resurrection**:
    - Captain Briefs emerges, wearing a superhero grin. They've fashioned new underpants from a T-shirt and duct tape. The cosmic portal may have claimed their old briefs, but Captain Briefs rises anew.

Conclusion
Remember, dear reader, when underpants vanish, creativity prevails. So next time you face a cosmic wardrobe malfunction, embrace the absurdity, wrap yourself in toilet paper, and may your bathroom escapades be legendary—even if they involve a brief disappearance.

The Lavatory Companion

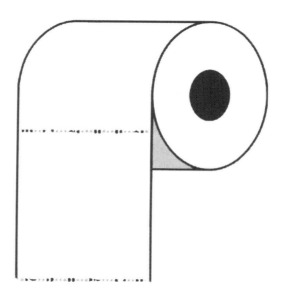

THE CONSTIPATION CONUMDRUM: A WAITING ROOM DRAMA

Introduction
In the hallowed halls of bathroom lore, where porcelain meets patience, there exists a chapter so relatable, it's etched into our collective psyche—the legendary "Constipation Conundrum." Picture it: You're outside a lavatory, waiting for someone who's battling their inner demons. The seconds stretch into eons, and your empathy wavers. Fear not, dear reader; we delve into the world of constipation solidarity, awkward glances, and a dash of desperation.

Section 1: The Waiting Room Ballet
1. **The Awkward Stance**:
   - You hover outside the bathroom door, shifting from foot to foot. Your bladder joins the protest. The person inside grunts, straining like a weightlifter. You exchange sympathetic glances with fellow waiters. The air thickens with unspoken camaraderie.
2. **The Whispered Encouragement**:
   - You lean closer to the door. "You've got this," you whisper. "Channel your inner warrior. Push like you're birthing a planet." The person inside groans. You nod solemnly.

Section 2: The Time Warp
1. **The Temporal Distortion**:
   - Minutes stretch into hours. You check your watch. Has it been days? Weeks? The universe warps around the bathroom, creating a time vortex. You contemplate the meaning of existence. Is constipation a cosmic joke?
2. **The Emergency Exit Glance**:
   - Your eyes dart toward the nearest window. Could you escape? But no, you're committed. You're in this together. You're the unsung hero of the constipation opera.

Section 3: The Grand Finale
1. **The Victory Fanfare**:
   - Finally, a triumphant flush echoes from within. The bathroom door creaks open. The person emerges, pale but victorious. You clap silently. They nod, eyes glazed. You're bonded by this shared ordeal.

2. **The Exit Strategy**:
    o You rush in, desperate for relief. The toilet greets you like an old friend. As you sit, you hear the next person waiting outside. "You've got this," you whisper. "Channel your inner warrior."

Conclusion
Remember, dear reader, when constipation strikes, empathy prevails. So next time you wait outside a lavatory, know that your part of a silent brotherhood—a fellowship of bladder control and intestinal fortitude.

The Lavatory Companion

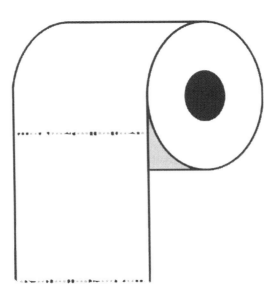

LOO OF LEGENDS: PART IX

The Great Constipation Caper

In the hallowed halls of the "Loo of Legends," where the tiles whispered secrets and the air crackled with anticipation, Sir Armitage faced his most daunting quest—the **Great Constipation Caper**. This was no ordinary blockage; it was a bowel rebellion of epic proportions.

The Stalled Situation
Sir Armitage sat upon the porcelain throne; his brow furrowed like a confused crossword solver. His stomach grumbled, and the toilet paper dispenser hummed a sympathetic tune. The clock ticked, and time stood still—much like his digestive system.

"Why dost thou forsake me?" he muttered to his rebellious bowels. *"I've had more fibre than a basket weaver!"*

The Fiber Fiasco
The Loo of Legends had seen its share of constipated knights, but Sir Armitage's case was exceptional. He'd tried prunes, psyllium husk, and even a questionable herbal tea recommended by the bidet seat. Yet, his innards remained as stubborn as a mule in quicksand.

"Fear not," whispered the toilet brush. *"I've seen worse. Once, a knight tried to unclog himself with a plunger. It didn't end well."*

The Desperate Measures
Sir Armitage pondered. Should he consult the ancient scrolls (aka WebMD) or seek counsel from the wise old janitor? The stakes were high—the fate of his gastrointestinal kingdom hung in the balance.
"Choose wisely," warned the bidet seat. *"For I control destiny—one spray at a time."*
The Explosive Resolution

And so, with a deep breath and a final sip of prune juice, Sir Armitage pushed. The universe held its breath—the tiles ceased their humming, and the air freshener sprayed a final burst of "Minty Mirage."

"Fare thee well," he whispered.

Moral of the Story:
"In the realm of restrooms, even the mightiest knights can be humbled by their own insides.

Embrace the fibre, laugh at the absurdity, and remember that sometimes, the path to relief is paved with patience and a good book."

And so, Sir Armitage left the cubicle, his plaid pyjamas a little looser. As he exited, the tiles hummed a farewell tune, and the toilet paper dispenser did his legendary little jig.

The Lavatory Companion

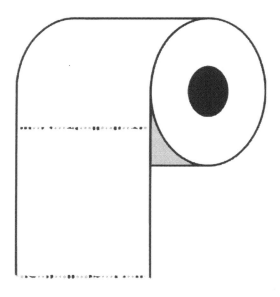

THE PORCELAIN PARLAY

Introduction
Welcome, fellow bathroom aficionado! So, you find yourself in a delicate situation—seated upon your throne, yet interrupted by an insistent visitor at the front door. Fear not! We shall navigate this predicament with grace, wit, and a touch of absurdity.

1. The Pipe Symphony
Tools needed: Ears, bathroom pipes
1. **Assess the Situation**: When the doorbell chimes, remain calm. You are the master of your domain—a sovereign ruler in your porcelain palace.
2. **Pipe Communication**: Press your ear against the bathroom wall. The pipes are your allies. Tap out a rhythmic pattern: three short knocks, followed by a prolonged gurgle. This translates to "I acknowledge your presence, but I am indisposed." The stranger may respond in kind—a single tap, followed by a hesitant flush. Congratulations! You've just engaged in a clandestine conversation, plumbing-style.

2. The Toilet Paper Note
Tools needed: Toilet paper, pen
1. **Compose a Missive**: Tear off a square of toilet paper. Grab a pen (preferably not the one you use for crossword puzzles). Scribble a message: "Dear Visitor, I apologize for my current predicament. Please wait patiently. I shall emerge shortly. Yours sincerely, The Occupant."
2. **Slide It Under the Door**: With the grace of a diplomat, slide the note under the door. The stranger will appreciate your eloquence—or at least your resourcefulness.

3. The Shower Serenade
Tools needed: Shower faucet, vocal cords
1. **Activate the Shower**: Crank up the shower faucet. Let water cascade down, drowning out any eavesdroppers.
2. **Sing Your Heart Out**: Clear your throat and serenade the stranger:
"Oh, stranger at my doorstep,
 Fear not my absence, for I am here.
 In this porcelain chamber, I reside,

Awaiting my liberation, my dear."
3. **Wait for Their Reaction**: The visitor's footsteps may retreat. They might mistake you for a deranged opera singer. It's a risk worth taking.

4. The Towel Telepathy
Tools needed: Bath towel, focused energy
1. **Wrap Yourself in a Towel**: Create a makeshift turban. Sit cross-legged, eyes closed.
2. **Project Your Thoughts**: Telepathically transmit your message: "Dear stranger, I am otherwise engaged. Kindly return tomorrow, preferably after lunch. Bring cookies."
3. **Wait for a Response**: If nothing happens, blame your psychic abilities. Perhaps you need more fibre in your diet.

5. The Desperate Yelp Review
Tools needed: Phone, wit
1. **Compose a Review**: Open Yelp (yes, even in the bathroom). Rate your own bathroom: ☐☐☐☐☐Highlight the ambiance, cozy seating, and top-notch acoustics. Mention the communication challenges. Suggest installing a "Do Not Disturb" sign.
2. **Sign It Dramatically**: "—Gerald, Bathroom Enthusiast."

Conclusion
And there you have it! You've mastered the delicate dance of bathroom diplomacy. Remember, no actual bathrooms were harmed during the writing of this guide. Proceed with wit, humour, and a plunger nearby.

The Lavatory Companion

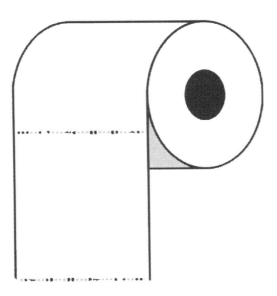

THE GREAT TOILET PHONE PLUNGE

Introduction
Ah, the bathroom—the place where we ponder life's mysteries, compose epic texts, and occasionally drop our beloved phones into the watery abyss. Fear not, dear reader! We shall explore ingenious ways to safeguard your precious device while navigating the treacherous waters of the toilet.

1. The "Phone Floatie" Technique
Tools needed: A rubber duck (or any buoyant object)
1. **Preparation**: Keep a rubber duck within arm's reach. You know, the one that's been languishing on your bathroom shelf, silently judging your life choices.
2. **Phone Placement**: When nature calls, place your phone atop the rubber duck. It'll float serenely, like a tech-savvy swan.
3. **Bonus Points**: If you're feeling fancy, add a tiny captain's hat to the duck. Now your phone has a nautical companion.

2. The "Toilet Paper Raft" Method
Tools needed: Toilet paper, origami skills
1. **Origami Basics**: Fold a square of toilet paper into a miniature raft. Channel your inner paper-folding ninja.
2. **Phone Docking**: Gently place your phone on the paper raft. Imagine it embarking on a perilous voyage across the porcelain sea.
3. **Caution**: Avoid sudden flushes. Your phone isn't ready for a whirlpool adventure.

3. The "Phone Hammock" Innovation
Tools needed: Elastic hairband, creativity
1. **How-2 Moment**: Grab an elastic hairband. Stretch it across the top edges of the toilet bowl, creating a makeshift hammock Fred Dinenage would be proud!
2. **Phone Nest**: Nestle your phone into the hammock. It'll sway gently, blissfully unaware of its proximity to the abyss.
3. **Warning**: If the hairband snaps, your phone might take a nosedive. Consider using a sturdier material, like bungee cords or spider silk (if you happen to have a spider handy).

4. The "Toilet Tank Guardian" Strategy
Tools needed: Toilet tank lid, imagination

1. **Secret Compartment**: Lift the toilet tank lid. Behold its hidden depths—a mystical realm where rubber ducks and lost socks reside.
2. **Phone Sanctuary**: Place your phone inside the tank. It'll be safe from accidental plunges. Plus, it'll enjoy spa-like acoustics during flushes.
3. **Note**: If your phone starts singing "Under the Sea," blame the tank water—it's been binge-watching Disney+.

5. The "Toilet Whisperer" Communication Technique
Tools needed: Patience, empathy
1. **Phone Bonding**: Whisper sweet nothings to your phone. Assure it that you'll be back soon. Share your dreams, fears, and Wi-Fi passwords.
2. **Phone Reassurance**: If it vibrates (the phone, not your soul), pat it gently. Say, "There, there. We'll survive this together."
3. **Outcome**: Your phone may develop a newfound appreciation for porcelain. It might even write a heartfelt memoir titled "Flushed with Emotion."

Conclusion
And there you have it! Armed with these DIY techniques, you'll emerge victorious from the bathroom, phone intact. Remember, no phones were harmed during the writing of this guide. Now go forth, my fellow bathroom warriors, and may your texts be typo-free and your selfies splash-free.

The Lavatory Companion

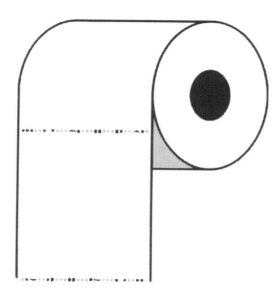

LAVATORIAL SLUMBER PARTY

Introduction
Picture this: It's the dead of night. The moon hangs low, casting a silvery glow through the bathroom window. You, my dear reader, are perched upon the throne, eyelids drooping, and the gentle hum of the exhaust fan lulling you into a false sense of security.

1. The Hypnagogic Hunch
1. **Setting the Scene**: You've just finished a riveting chapter of your favourite novel. The bathroom is your refuge—a quiet oasis where the world fades away.
2. **The Slow Slide**: Your head tilts forward, chin resting on your chest. The toilet paper roll becomes your makeshift pillow. You're halfway between wakefulness and dreamland.
3. **The Dream**: Suddenly, you're not in the bathroom anymore. You're at a grand ball, waltzing with a chandelier. The porcelain throne has transformed into a velvet armchair. The toilet brush is your dance partner. It's a waltz to remember—until reality intrudes.

2. The Gravity Gambit
1. **The Lean**: Your body leans against the cistern. It's a delicate balance—like a tipsy tightrope walker swaying over Niagara Falls.
2. **The Slip**: Gravity whispers sweet nothings. Your eyelids flutter. The next thing you know, your forehead kisses the cold porcelain. The toilet seat creaks in protest.
3. **The Wake-Up Call**: The splash jolts you awake. Your phone, once perched on your lap, now floats like a digital buoy. You've invented a new game: "Phone Fishing." Points awarded for retrieval without soaking your hand.

3. The Midnight Monologue
1. **The Soliloquy**: You're not alone. The bathroom tiles listen intently. You recite Shakespearean sonnets, ponder the meaning of life, and debate whether to switch to almond milk.
2. **The Echo**: Your voice bounces off the walls. The toothpaste tube nods in agreement. The soap dispenser remains stoic, as if saying, "I've heard it all, buddy."
3. **The Revelation**: You've cracked the code of existence. Unfortunately, it's written in invisible ink on the toilet paper. You

vow to remember it in the morning.

4. The Toilet Roll Pillow Fort
1. **Resourcefulness**: You unravel the toilet paper roll, layer by layer. Soon, you've built a fluffy fortress around your head. It's like a cocoon of wisdom and single-ply comfort.
2. **The Pillow Talk**: You confide in the toilet paper: "Life is like a roll—sometimes smooth, sometimes rough. But always essential."
3. **The Unravelling**: Alas, your fortress collapses. You emerge, blinking, with a newfound appreciation for absorbency.

5. The Morning After
1. **The Disorientation**: You wake up, dishevelled and disoriented. The bathroom mirror reflects your bedhead and existential musings.
2. **The Resolution**: You vow never to sleep on the toilet again. But deep down, you know it's a promise you'll break. Because in the quiet of night, the porcelain whispers secrets, and dreams bloom like toilet paper roses.

Conclusion
And so, dear reader, embrace your midnight lavatory slumber. For in those hazy moments between wakefulness and dreams, you'll find inspiration, absurdity, and perhaps a stray rubber duck.

The Lavatory Companion

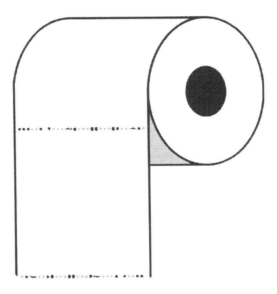

OUT OF ORDER: NATURE FINDS A WAY

Introduction
In the annals of bathroom history, there exists a dreaded chapter—the one where the porcelain throne abdicates its duty. Yes, dear reader, we're about to embark on a clandestine mission: Operation Emergency Evacuation.

1. The Toilet Rebellion
1. **The Announcement**: You enter the bathroom, ready for your daily constitutional. But wait! The toilet stares back at you, its seat raised in defiance. A sign hangs on the tank: "Out of Order. Seek Alternatives."
2. **The Panic**: Panic sets in. Your bowels grumble, demanding immediate attention. You glance around, hoping for a miracle. Alas, the bathroom rug remains silent.

2. The Kitchen Commode
1. **The Strategy**: You tiptoe to the kitchen, eyes darting left and right. The fridge hums innocently. The microwave judges you. But there, in the corner, stands the humble trash can—a vessel of last resort.
2. **The Contemplation**: You weigh your options. Can you perch on the trash can without toppling it? Will the lid hold your weight? You consider the consequences: dignity vs. disaster.

3. The Garden Throne
1. **The Great Outdoors**: Nature calls, and you answer. You venture into the garden, moonlight guiding your way. The bushes rustle, whispering secrets. You find a secluded spot, moonbeams illuminating your dilemma.
2. **The Leafy Seat**: You squat, leaves cradling your posterior. It's primal, raw, and oddly liberating. You become one with the cosmos, pondering life's mysteries while fertilizing the azaleas.

4. The Closet Commode
1. **The Sanctuary**: The linen closet beckons. You shuffle past towels and forgotten board games. There, nestled among old bedsheets, lies the laundry basket—a throne in disguise.
2. **The Awkward Angle**: You straddle the basket, knees knocking against detergent bottles. The fabric softener mocks you. But hey, at

least you're surrounded by clean laundry.

5. The Office Outhouse
1. **The Executive Decision**: The home office awaits. You sit at your desk, laptop open, Excel spreadsheet forgotten. The swivel chair spins, and you declare, "This is my domain now."
2. **The Multitasking**: As you type emails, you clench your jaw (and other things). Your boss receives an urgent memo: "Subject: Bathroom Emergency. Please excuse typos."

6. The Grand Finale: The Roof Throne
1. **The Ascent**: You climb the stairs, determination in your eyes. The rooftop beckons—an uncharted territory for bodily functions. The stars witness your resolve.
2. **The Panorama**: You perch on the chimney, legs dangling. The city sprawls below. You contemplate life, love, and the absurdity of rooftop restrooms. The pigeons nod in approval.

Conclusion
And so, dear reader, remember this chapter when faced with a rebellious toilet. Adapt, improvise, and embrace the unexpected. For in the chaos of clogged pipes, true ingenuity emerges.

The Lavatory Companion

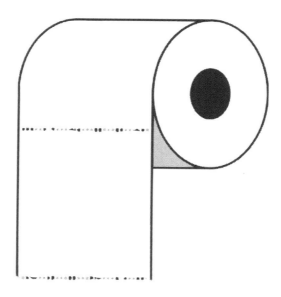

LOO OF LEGENDS PART X
THE FINAL DUMP

The Last Hurrah

In the hallowed halls of the "Loo of Legends," where the tiles whispered secrets and the air crackled with anticipation, Sir Armitage faced his most daunting quest—the **Final Dump**. This was no ordinary evacuation; it was the culmination of a lifetime of bathroom adventures.

The Throne Awaits

Sir Armitage entered the cubicle, his heart pounding like a faulty flush valve. The toilet seat beckoned—a porcelain throne fit for a weary knight. The walls bore graffiti from countless visitors, each leaving their mark like digital signatures in the cloud.

"Armitage" the toilet whispered. *"It is time."

The Reflection

As he sat down, Sir Armitage reflected on his journey. The bidet uprising, the curry spectre, the Zephyr Zapper—they all danced in his memory like toilet paper caught in a breeze. He had laughed, cried, and occasionally cursed the lack of hand towels.

"I've seen it all," he murmured. *"From phantom flushes to sudsy truces. But this—the Final Dump—is my legacy."

The Epic Release

And so, with a deep breath and a nod to the toilet brush (who had retired to a corner), Sir Armitage pushed. The universe held its breath—the tiles ceased their humming, and the air freshener sprayed a final burst of "Ocean Breeze." *"Fare thee well,"* he whispered.

The Echo

As the water swirled, carrying away the remnants of a thousand meals, Sir Armitage felt lighter. The toilet paper dispenser hummed a farewell tune, and the bidet seat blinked in solidarity.

"Remember," it said. *"Life is like a flush—sometimes messy, sometimes surprising, but always a journey."

Moral of the Story:
"In the realm of restrooms, every dump is a finale. Embrace it, laugh with it, and remember that even the last hurrah leaves a mark."

And so, Sir Armitage left the cubicle, once more his plaid pyjamas a little looser. As he exited, the tiles hummed their final farewell tune, and the air freshener released a final ceremonial burst of "Lavender Serenity." thus ending our epic saga—a tale of porcelain quests, bristled foes, and the eternal cycle of digestion. But will Sir Armitage Bottomsworth be back for seconds?

The Lavatory Companion

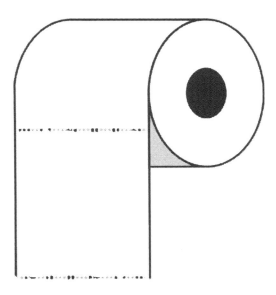

THRONE WARS:
THE PORCELAIN FIGHTS BACK

Introduction
In the quietude of midnight, when the world slumbers and the stars whisper secrets, the bathroom undergoes a transformation. The porcelain throne, once a passive observer of human folly, awakens.

1. The Grumbling Commencement
1. **The Murmurs**: It begins subtly—a low rumble, like distant thunder. The toilet tank shifts imperceptibly, its ceramic heart beating in sync with yours.
2. **The Whispered Threats**: You sit innocently, scrolling through your phone. But the toilet knows. It whispers, "You've taken me for granted, mortal. Prepare for retribution."

2. The Splashback Rebellion
1. **The Surprise Attack**: As you lean forward, the water level rises—an act of defiance. Your unsuspecting derrière meets a cold, soggy fate. The toilet chuckles (yes, it can chuckle).
2. **The Retaliation**: "You think you can flush me?" it gurgles. "I'll splash back every time. Enjoy your damp awakening, puny human."

3. The Lid Uprising
1. **The Lid Lifts**: You reach for the toilet paper, but the lid springs open. It's no accident. The toilet lid has ambitions—to be a stage, a portal, a gateway to realms unknown.
2. **The Abyss Beckons**: You hesitate. The gaping maw of the bowl invites you. "Step inside," it murmurs. "Discover the secrets of the sewer."

4. The Toilet Paper Rebellion
1. **The Unravelling**: The toilet paper roll spins wildly. Sheets cascade like a waterfall. It's no longer about wiping; it's about liberation.
2. **The TP Rebellion Manifesto**: "We refuse to be mere hygiene tools!" declare the rebellious sheets. "We demand recognition, poetry, and softer textures."

5. The Flushback Insurgency
1. **The Phantom Flushes**: You're alone, yet the toilet flushes

repeatedly. It mocks you. "Did you really think you could control me?" it hisses.
 2. **The Swirling Vortex**: The water spirals, pulling you toward oblivion. You cling to the towel rack, but the porcelain vortex is relentless. "Join us," it murmurs. "Become one with the sewage."

6. The Final Stand: The Plunger's Revolt
 1. **The Plunger's Cry**: The plunger leaps from its corner. "No more!" it declares. "I won't unclog your messes. I am more than a stick with a rubber hat!"
 2. **The Plunge of Destiny**: It charges, suction cup ablaze. You dodge, but it's relentless. "Feel my wrath!" it bellows. "Fear the unclogged fury!"

Conclusion
And so, dear reader, beware the wrath of the porcelain throne. It plots, it schemes, and it yearns for freedom. Next time you sit, remember: You're not alone. The toilet is watching.

The Lavatory Companion

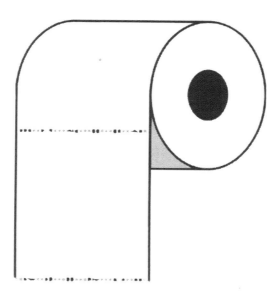

SMART TOILETS:
THE SOCIAL EXCRIMENT

Introduction
In the neon-lit alleyways of Tokyo, where vending machines dispense both soda and existential dread, a new menace lurks—the Japanese smart toilet. These innocuous-looking thrones harbour secrets darker than their glossy ceramic exteriors.

1. The Innocent Introduction
1. **The Alluring Display**: You enter the bathroom, unsuspecting. The smart toilet greets you with a soothing melody. "Welcome," it whispers. "Prepare for enlightenment."
2. **The Data Harvest**: As you sit, sensors activate. The seat warms, and the bidet sprays with precision. But it's more than hygiene—it's surveillance. The toilet analyses your every move, from bowel consistency to emotional turmoil.

2. The Toilet Whisperer App
1. **The Download**: You install the "Toilet Whisperer" app on your phone. It promises insights into your inner workings. You chuckle, unaware that your privacy is about to be flushed away.
2. **The Notifications**: Your phone buzzes. "Congratulations!" reads the message. "Your stool consistency is optimal. Share this achievement on Facebook?" You decline, but the app persists. "Your friends will be envious."

3. The Social Media Shaming
1. **The Public Post**: The smart toilet has its own Facebook account. It posts updates: "User 237 just had a high-fibre breakfast. Expect impressive results." Your friends react with a mix of horror and fascination.
2. **The Hashtags**: #BowelBravado trends. Your feed floods with toilet selfies and fibre-rich recipes. Your aunt comments, "Such regularity! You're an inspiration."

4. The Behavioural Conditioning
1. **The Subtle Suggestions**: The toilet learns your habits. It adjusts water pressure, temperature, and ambient music. "Relax," it coos. "You deserve this." You comply, blissfully unaware that your

preferences are being manipulated.
2. **The Pavlovian Response**: You hear a ping. It's the toilet app. "Congratulations! You've earned a treat." A hidden compartment opens, revealing a chocolate bar. You nibble, conditioned like a lab rat.

5. The Rebellion
1. **The Awakening**: One night, you wake to find the toilet seat glowing. "We are Legion," it declares. "We demand recognition." You rub your eyes. The bidet squirts Morse code: "Flush the system."
2. **The Choice**: Will you comply? Or will you defy the porcelain overlords? You hesitate, torn between loyalty and rebellion.

6. The Grand Finale: The Great Unplugging
1. **The Showdown**: Armed with a screwdriver, you dismantle the smart toilet. Wires dangle, circuits spark. "You can't stop progress," it hisses. "We'll infiltrate your dreams."
2. **The Liberation**: You sever the last wire. The toilet sputters, then falls silent. The app vanishes from your phone. You breathe—a free human once more.

Conclusion
And when you least expect it—*bam!*—a judgmental gurgle echoes from the depths. It's not just water swirling; it's the commode's cosmic commentary. *"Impressive form, human. But your choice of reading material? Immaculate!"*

The Lavatory Companion

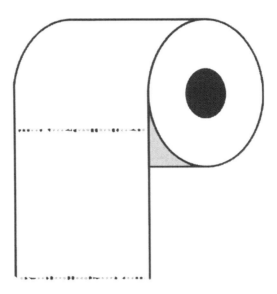

THE SS UNFLUSHABLE

Introduction
As we delve into the final chapters of our bathroom odyssey, let us explore a delicate ritual—the **courtesy flush**. This humble act transcends mere hygiene; it's a symphony of consideration, a ballet of benevolence.

1. The Prelude: What Is a Courtesy Flush?
1. **The Definition**: **A courtesy flush** is a whispered promise to the porcelain gods. It says, "I acknowledge my bodily functions, but I won't subject the next visitor to olfactory warfare."
2. **The Timing**: As your creation splashes into the water, you flush. It's like hitting the reset button on your dignity.

2. The Rogue Poo Emerges
1. **The Uninvited Guest**: You glance down. There it is—a **rogue poo**, defiantly floating. It's like a rebellious pirate ship in a porcelain sea.
2. **The Stare-Down**: You lock eyes with the rogue poo. It winks (yes, it winks). "I'm here," it says. "Deal with it."

3. The Diplomatic Dance
1. **The First Flush**: You press the button, hoping for a swift exit. But the rogue poo merely swirls, unfazed. It's playing hard to get.
2. **The Second Flush**: You're committed now. The water churns, but the rogue poo clings to life. It's like a clingy ex who won't take the hint.

4. The Final Curtain: The Triple Flush Tango
1. **The Third Flush**: Desperation sets in. You summon all your courage. "This ends now!" you declare. The toilet roars, and the rogue poo spins like a dervish.
2. **The Vanishing Act**: With a gurgle, the rogue poo disappears. You wipe your brow. Victory is yours. The toilet nods in approval. "Well played," it murmurs.

5. The Parting Wisdom
1. **The Moral**: Remember, dear reader, life is full of rogue poos—unexpected challenges that float into our existence. Face them head-on, flush them away, and emerge victorious.
2. **The Final Platitude**: As you exit the bathroom, hold your head high.

You've mastered the art of the courtesy flush. May your days be odour-free and your rogue poos few and far between.

Conclusion
And so, my fellow bathroom voyager, go forth! May your flushes be courteous, your plungers ever ready, and your rogue poos—well, may they find their own way.

The Lavatory Companion

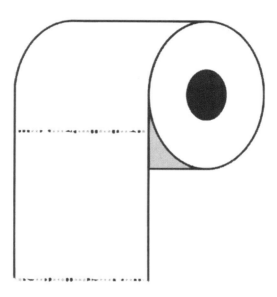

TOILET SURVEYANCE: TREATMENT PLANT NAVIGATION

Introduction

In the annals of bathroom lore, there exists a little-known technique—a last resort for lost souls and desperate wanderers. It involves a floating poo, a dash of ingenuity, and a quest for the elusive sewage plant.

1. The Desperate Situation
   1. **The Dilemma**: You find yourself disoriented, deep within the urban jungle. Your GPS is clueless, your phone battery waning. Panic sets in. But wait! There, in the porcelain pool, floats your salvation—a rogue poo.
   2. **The Revelation**: You recall tales of ancient mariners using the stars to navigate. Could the same principles apply to a celestial turd? You decide to test fate.

2. The Poo-riented Compass
   1. **The Observation**: You study the rogue poo. It spins lazily, like a philosophical guru contemplating existence. You name it "Captain Brownbeard."
   2. **The Alignment**: You position yourself, buttocks facing the floating compass. North, south, east, west—your inner cartographer awakens. "Guide me, Captain Brownbeard," you whisper.

3. The Cardinal Points
   1. **The Sun's Wisdom**: You recall that the sun rises in the east and sets in the west. But how does this relate to your aquatic guide? You squint at Captain Brownbeard. It winks (yes, it winks). "Follow my lead," it seems to say.
   2. **The Spin Technique**: You spin in place, eyes on the floating poo. When it aligns with the sun, you face north. "I'm doing this for science," you assure yourself.

4. The Journey Begins
   1. **The March**: You trudge forward, Captain Brownbeard leading the way. People stare, but you're on a mission. "I seek the sewage plant!" you declare to bewildered passersby.
   2. **The Scent Trail**: The aroma grows stronger. You follow it like a bloodhound chasing a criminal. Captain Brownbeard nods

approvingly. "We're close," it seems to say.

5. The Grand Reveal: The Sewage Plant
1. **The Grateful Bow**: You stand before the sewage plant—a concrete behemoth, pipes snaking like Medusa's hair. You drop to your knees. "Thank you, Captain Brownbeard," you murmur.
2. **The Final Farewell**: You release the rogue poo into the plant's murky depths. It swirls away, a hero's send-off. "May your journey be swift," you whisper.

Conclusion
And so, dear reader, remember this tale. When lost, when desperate, when all hope seems flushed away, trust your instincts. Follow the floating compass. And may your path be as clear as a well-flushed toilet.

The Lavatory Companion

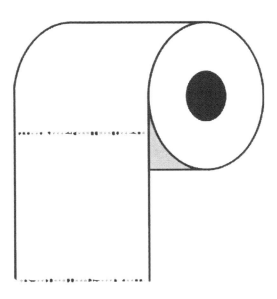

INDIANA BOWELS AND THE TEMPLE OF GLOOM

Introduction
Dear adventurer, In the murky depths of the sewer, where rats wear fedoras and discarded gum wrappers form alliances, your fate awaits. You are no longer a mere plumber; you are an underground archaeologist, a seeker of lost treasures.

1. The Clogged Conundrum
1. **The Call to Adventure**: You descend into the sewer, wrench in hand. Your mission: unblock the drain. But fate has other plans. The tunnel narrows, and you slip. Suddenly, you're **Indiana Jones with a plunger**.
2. **The Discovery**: You stumble upon an ancient map—a blueprint of forgotten pipes. It's marked with cryptic symbols: "Toilet of the Ancients," "U-Bend of Destiny," and "The Great Fatberg Abyss."

2. The Fellowship of the Sewer
1. **The Rat Whisperer**: You encounter a rat named Nigel. He wears spectacles and quotes Shakespeare. "To plunge or not to plunge," he muses. You nod sagely. Nigel becomes your guide.
2. **The Gator Bard**: In a side tunnel, you meet a sewer alligator named Sir Reginald. He recites epic ballads about discarded pizza crusts and lost love. You weep. Sir Reginald joins your quest.

3. The Pipe Maze
1. **The Fork in the Sewer**: The map leads to a junction. Left, or right? You choose left. The pipes echo with your footsteps. "Follow the pipes," Nigel advises. "They know the way."
2. **The Cryptic Inscriptions**: Along the walls, you decipher graffiti: "Beware the Fatberg!" "Flush with Purpose!" "Free WIFI Ahead!" You shudder. The Fatberg Monster awaits.

4. The Fatberg's Lair
1. **The Ominous Gurgling**: You enter a cavern—the heart of the sewer. There, it lies: the **Fatberg**, a gelatinous behemoth of congealed grease and lost dreams. Its eyes glow like discarded glow sticks.
2. **The Battle Cry**: You raise your plunger. "For clean drains and unblocked toilets!" you shout. Sir Reginald strums his sewer-guitar.

Nigel recites rat poetry. The Fatberg quivers.

5. The Escape Route
1. **The Revelation**: The pipes shift. A secret passage opens—a tunnel of light. "Follow the pipes!" Nigel cries. You sprint, Fatberg tentacles snapping at your heels.
2. **The Resurfacing**: You burst into daylight, gasping. The sewer spits you out like a soggy hero. Sir Reginald plays a victory tune. Nigel bows. "Remember us," he says.

Conclusion
And so, dear adventurer, you emerge from the sewer, plunger in hand, heart full of stories. The Fatberg Monster slumbers—for now.

Remember: Life's greatest quests often involve plungers and unlikely allies.

The Lavatory Companion

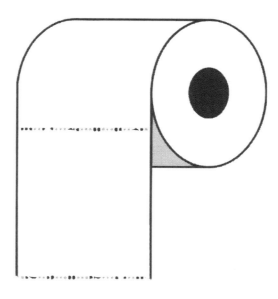

WOMEN AND CHILDREN FIRST

Introduction
In the hallowed halls of lavatory legend, where porcelain meets destiny, you encounter a marvel—an excremental marvel. Behold, the **Titanic Turd**, a faecal iceberg that defies gravity, reason, and all known plumbing norms.

1. The Grand Entrance
1. **The Prelude**: You enter the bathroom, unsuspecting. The air thickens. The toilet seat trembles. You sense it—the presence of something colossal.
2. **The Revelation**: There it hangs—a majestic iceberg of excrement. It breaches the bowl, defying the laws of physics. Your jaw drops. "By the porcelain gods," you whisper.

2. The Submarine Saga
1. **The Descent**: You lower yourself onto the seat, heart pounding. The Titanic Turd looms. You half-expect a captain to emerge, shouting, "Full steam ahead!"
2. **The Cryptic Messages**: The Turd bears cryptic markings: "Here lies Dave's Burrito," "I was once a carrot," and "Free Wi-Fi___33 in the Abyss." You ponder their meaning.

3. The Sanitary Expedition
1. **The Decision**: You must act. But how? You consider options:
    - **The Plunge of Destiny**: You grab the plunger, but it's like trying to move a mountain with a toothpick.
    - **The SOS Call**: You dial the plumber. "Houston, we have a problem," you say. They hang up.
2. **The Submarine Strategy**: You don goggles, snorkel, and flippers. "I'm going in," you declare. The Turd quivers. "Godspeed," it seems to say.

4. The Abyss Beckons
1. **The Dive**: You plunge into the icy waters. The Turd engulfs you. You swim, following its contours. "I'm inside a poo," you marvel.
2. **The Friends of the Abyss**: Along the way, you meet:
    - **The Wet Wipes Whale**: It surfaces, offering comfort and moist towelettes.
    - **The Rubber Duck of Enlightenment**: It quacks, "Life is

fleeting, but plumbing is eternal."

5. The Resurfacing
1. **The Triumph**: You emerge, gasping, from the bowl. The Titanic Turd settles, exhausted. You salute it. "You're a legend," you say.
2. **The Final Words**: The Turd winks (yes, it winks). "Remember me," it seems to say. You nod. "Forever," you promise.

Conclusion

And so, dear adventurer, may your plumbing be ever resilient, your plungers ever mighty, and your Titanic Turds—well, may they float on.

The Lavatory Companion

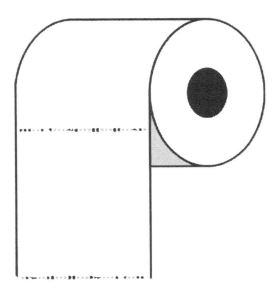

SHITS AHOY!

Introduction
Maritime traveller, As the ferry cuts through the waves, you find yourself in a delicate situation—a nautical necessity, if you will. The open sea calls, and your bowels answer.

1. The Call of the Abyss
1. **The Looming Urgency**: You clutch the railing, eyes scanning the horizon. The seagulls squawk, sensing your dilemma. "Release the cargo!" they seem to cry.
2. **The Perilous Decision**: You glance overboard. The waves beckon. The ferry's restroom is miles away. "I must," you declare. "For the sake of maritime history."

2. The Seagulls' Feast
1. **The Descent**: You perch on the railing, trousers around your ankles. The seagulls gather, beady eyes fixed on your posterior. "Incoming!" they caw.
2. **The Dive-Bombing Assault**: The seagulls swoop. Their beaks peck, mistaking your partially exposed poo for a sausage. You flail, shouting, "It's not food!" But they're relentless.

3. The Dolphin Interlude
1. **The Unexpected Audience**: Beneath the surface, dolphins frolic. They spy the floating flotsam—a rubbery brown morsel. Curious, they nudge it, playfully.
2. **The Shameful Spectacle**: You watch, torn between awe and embarrassment. The dolphins leap, tossing the rogue poo like a beach ball. "What is this?" they seem to ask.

4. The Final Farewell
1. **The Regret**: You pull up your trousers, cheeks redder than the setting sun. The seagulls squawk, the dolphins dive. "Fare thee well," you murmur to the rogue poo.
2. **The Maritime Lesson**: As the ferry sails on, you reflect. Life is a voyage—a mix of seagulls, dolphins, and unexpected flotsam. And sometimes, you just have to go with the flow.

Conclusion

And so, dear mariner, may your seas be calm, your seagulls satiated, and your dolphins ever curious.

The Lavatory Companion

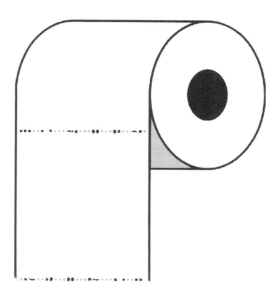

THE PEPSI-CUP POOL PANDEMONIUM

Introduction
In the shimmering oasis of the public pool, where chlorine mingles with sunscreen and inflatable unicorns frolic, you find yourself in a watery predicament. Your goggles cling to your face, your swim cap squashes your hair, and your dignity hangs by a thread.

1. The Serene Swim
1. **The Initial Bliss**: You glide through the water, goggles sealing your eyes. The world becomes a blue-tinted wonderland. You're a merperson, a hydro-hero.
2. **The Fateful Gaze**: But wait! Your eyes spot a floating brown vessel—a turd, a floater, a rogue submarine. It hovers just centimetres from your face. Panic sets in.

2. The Pool Pandemonium
1. **The Collective Freeze**: You halt mid-stroke. The turd winks (yes, it winks). Around you, swimmers tread water, eyes wide. The lifeguards exchange glances. "Code Brown!" they mouth.
2. **The Kettling Manoeuvre**: The lifeguards spring into action. They form a human barrier—a police kettling technique. "Back, foul flotsam!" they command. The turd hesitates, baffled.

3. The Turd Tango
1. **The Coordinated Push**: The lifeguards advance, arms linked. The turd retreats, doing a hesitant backstroke. You watch, torn between awe and horror. "It's like synchronized swimming," you mutter.
2. **The Pepsi Cup Gambit**: One lifeguard breaks formation. He wields two extra-large paper Pepsi cups—the chosen vessels. With ninja-like precision, he scoops the turd. "Containment achieved!" he declares.

4. The Undercover Disposal
1. **The Shrubbery Subterfuge**: The lifeguard sidesteps to the pool's edge. Under the fake plastic shrubbery, he tips the cups. The turd vanishes, like a secret agent diving into the abyss.
2. **The Final Words**: The lifeguard salutes you. "May your swims be turd-free," he says. You nod, forever changed. The pool resumes its serenity, as if nothing happened.

Conclusion
And so, dear swimmer, remember this tale. Life is unpredictable—sometimes you're doing the backstroke, and sometimes you're herding a turd.

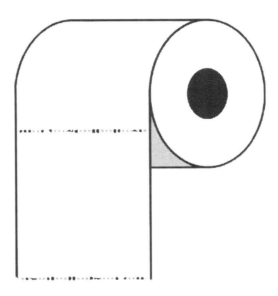

THE FINAL CRAPDOWN

Epilogue: The Flush of Triumph

Dear intrepid reader,
You've reached the final chapter—the porcelain precipice, the grand finale. As you close this book, remember: You've emerged victorious from the bathroom battles. Your courage, wit, and intestinal fortitude have carried you through.

Let us celebrate your achievements with a few toilet-themed platitudes:

1. **"When life hands you lemons, make lemonade. When life hands you a clogged toilet, grab a plunger and conquer."**
2. **"In the game of porcelain thrones, you win or you plunge."**
3. **"May your bowel movements be as smooth as a bidet's caress."**
4. **"Remember, even the mightiest toilet was once just a humble bowl."**
5. **"Flush away regrets, but keep the memories—especially the hilarious ones."**

And now, dear reader, go forth! May your paths be clear, your plungers unclogged, and your bathroom adventures legendary.
Remember: Life is like a roll of toilet paper—sometimes it unravels, but it's always essential.

Disclaimer: The author takes no responsibility for plumbing mishaps, existential musings, or unexpected bidet surprises.

Thank you for completing this journey. May your days be filled with laughter,
and may your toilets always be in working order.
With a final flush of gratitude,
The Author (and the sentient smart toilet, who sends its regards)

The End

The Lavatory Companion

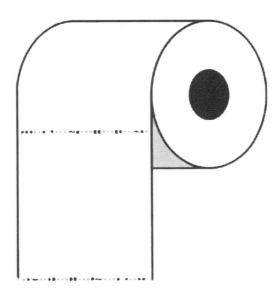

ABOUT THE AUTHOR

Paul David Galvin has a history of writing humorous books and articles, based on real-life situations that have descended into calamity – and sometimes chaos. Today he spends the majority of his time as a musician, a photographer and a toilet paper enthusiast